# Here Lies Kansas City

# Here Lies Kansas City

*A collection of our city's notables and their final resting places*

## Wilda Sandy

Hal Sandy
*photography*

**Bennett Schneider**
*Kansas City*

# Dedication

Without the 80 or so unique Kansas Citians
encapsulated herein, this book could not have been.
It is to them and their soaring spirit we
dedicate our efforts.

First Edition

All rights reserved 1984 Wilda and Hal Sandy

L. C. #84-51366   ISBN 0-918797-00-4

Printed in the Crown Colony of Hong Kong
by Mandarin Offset Marketing (HK) Ltd.

Published by Bennett Schneider Inc.
300 Ward Parkway Kansas City Missouri 64112 USA
816-531-8484

# Requiescat In Pace

Once upon *the* time, as friend Jane Flynn is wont to say, my husband Hal and I decided to write a book about Kansas City cemeteries, a show-and-tell of our town's past through its tombstones.

HERE LIES KANSAS CITY is the loving result. Within are profiles of 80 or so of our deceased who, for better or for worse, helped make Kansas City what it is today.

In selecting people to be included, we sought a cross-section of those whose influence on the town has been significant. We begin with the 1821 arrival of the young Francois Chouteaus from St. Louis, and we conclude with the late Sam Sosland who in 1983 left Kansas City richer by far than he found it.

In alphabetical sequence we go from Barney Allis of Hotel Muehlebach fame to John B. Wornall whose superb 1858 farmhouse is now a restored museum. In between are H. Roe Bartle and Johnny Lazia; Annie Chambers and William Rockhill Nelson; Mrs. A. Ross Hill and Satchel Paige; Ernest H. Newcomb and Ruth Seufert; Dr. Benoist Troost and Kathryn Winstead, of the legendary steakburger.

With the inevitable exceptions, *all* are buried here. The anomalies are Bereniece and Francois Chouteau, the earliest French family to come, settle, and eventually die here; and George Kessler, the gifted landscape architect who designed our exemplary parks and boulevard system at the turn-of-the-century. They are buried in St. Louis, yet are too major in our city's metamorphosis to leave out.

Another key figure in our town's being is Gabriel Prudhomme. His 257-acre farm on the river became in 1838 the *original townsite* of the Town Company of Kansas—in other words, Kansas City's cradle. After the 1880 closing of the old Catholic cemetery, where he was interred after reputedly being killed in a barroom brawl in 1831, his resting place becomes a mystery. But because he was pivotal, he's included, mystery and all.

Published materials and cemetery records differ in some instances. Where records and tombstones disagreed, tombstone dates were used. Thus Annie Chambers becomes two years younger than her obituary states and Col. John Harris, four. Tom Pendergast becomes one year older, and Elizabeth Epperson, who never told a soul her age, is revealed by her crypt inscription to have been eighty-four.

HERE LIES KANSAS CITY sketches our history through these disparate Kansas Citians. Meeting each of them helps explain a bit how we got the way we are. R.I.P.

WILDA SANDY

9

# People of Our Town

# Here Lies Kansas City

# Barney L. Allis

*1886-1962*

## The Muehlebach

It seems completely fitting that Barney Allis should have collapsed on the sidewalk just south of the Wyandotte street entrance to his beloved Muehlebach hotel the afternoon he died, April 17, 1962.

Seventy-six years earlier, in 1886, the man destined by grit, hard work and fight to become Kansas City's most famous hotelier was born in Poland. At age two he and his family immigrated to the United States. By the time Barney Allis was in his mid-forties, he'd already made his fortune.

Allis' immigrant father opened a tiny store on Fifth street, but the youngster entered the work-aday world on his own at a tender age. His saga is almost a textbook tale of rags to riches of the skinny little Pole who never grew taller than 5′ 3½″, who rose from newspaper hawker at the corner of 9th and Walnut streets to owner of his own printing shop to premier hotelier.

From printing, the metamorphosis to hotel-keeping was not the far stretch it might seem. His Allis Press printed "Tavern Talk," the mouth organ of the hotel industry hereabouts. The business contacts he made through that led him into the hotel trade.

Allis' first hotel venture soon after World War I was a partnership in Columbia, Missouri's Daniel Boone. In 1921, he became a partner in Joplin's late Connor hotel, which led to his purchasing stock in the Mid-Continent hotel chain here. This was top of the dial since Mid-Continent owned Kansas City's grand old Baltimore hotel and, what was to become Allis' flagship, the elegant Muehlebach.

Eventually he bought the Baltimore—the "dream hotel" of his less than privileged youth—as well as the Allis hotel in Wichita. Signs of the Great Depression triggered his selling these, and in 1931 putting all his bucks in the Muehlebach.

Touch and go it was, but Allis persevered. He survived the bleakest years of the 1930s and the War-spawned shortages of the 1940s to build his Muehlebach into the most prestigious hotel in the midwest. And in the doing, his name became synonymous with the hotel's. Big names filled its rooms and rosters, from Arthur Godfrey to Harry S Truman. And fittingly, Allis lived there too—in an antiques-furnished, walnut-paneled suite.

Barney Allis was one of Kansas City's big boosters. As vice-chairman of the Downtown committee, he prophetically said, "We can do anything if we've just got the vision and guts to go out and do it." Amen.

15

# Kirkland B. Armour

*1854-1901*

## Armour Packing Company

In 1870 Kirkland B. Armour and his brother Charles came to Kansas City from Chicago with their uncle Simeon B. Armour to take charge of the family's meat packing plant here. Sixteen years before on April 10, 1854, Armour was born in Stockbridge, New York to American blue-bloods whose forebears came early from England. After 31 years here, Kirk Armour would be gone, but far from forgotten in Kansas City.

The wealthy young man married and made his first home on prestigious Quality Hill. Appropriately so, since that high-toned residential neighborhood overlooked the source of his wealth in the West Bottoms below.

As the city moved south, the Kirk Armours followed. In 1896 they built a three-story palatial French chateau at Warwick and Armour boulevards (so named for his Uncle Simeon, a member of Kansas City's first Park Board.) The renowned architectural firm of Van Brunt and Howe designed Armour's splendid turreted red brick castle, one of many mansions lining both sides of that broad boulevard.

Kirk Armour was a handsome, mustachioed man, much dedicated to city betterment, the meat packing industry, and to fine livestock on the hoof. Active in forming the American Hereford Breeders Association, it was during his presidency that the group staged the first National Hereford Show here in 1899.

Armour prided himself on his thousand acre farm just south of today's Country Club district, and stocked it with cattle from England, which had once been part of the Queen's herd. Much altered, the old Armour farmhouse still stands at 6740 Pennsylvania avenue.

On September 27, 1901, the 47 year old Armour died. He was laid to rest in beautiful Elmwood where he had been a leading light in that cemetery's reorganization as a non-profit Society. He also served as the cemetery's first president.

The year following his death, Mrs. Armour built a charming and lasting memorial to him there—the small Gothic-style chapel of rough native stone and timber, visible from the cemetery's main entrance. Inside, the tiny sanctuary was finished with solid oak pews seating 85. From March 1904 when the first funeral was held there, the chapel was available for services. Now appropriately, an ecumenical Memorial Day service is held there each year. Both the chapel and the service are fitting, living tributes to Kirkland B. Armour who lies nearby.

17

# Mary Atkins

*1836-1911*

## Nelson-Atkins Museum of Art

Mary McAfee Atkins was an enigma to most people. A strangely reclusive former school teacher, she was widowed after a brief, late-in-life marriage to a childhood friend ten years her senior.

James Burris Atkins had come to Kansas City from their native Lawrenceburg, Kentucky in 1865. Here he engaged in milling, met the woman who became his first wife, married her, and was soon widowed, promising her never to remarry.

Atkins' business interests here turned to downtown real estate, and in short order he was a well-to-do man. It was following his first wife's death that the middle-aged widower resumed correspondence with Mary McAfee, his childhood friend in Kentucky. Setting aside the deathbed vow, he and Mary, then in her early forties, married in 1878, settled here at 905 McGee street.

Just eight years later Atkins died, a successful speculator whose estate amounted to a comfortable $250,000. Twenty-five years later when Mary Atkins died, she had neatly parlayed his nest egg into more than a million dollars.

Given to silence except among her few friends, a thrifty soul in the extreme, Mary Atkins expired on October 13, 1911, nine days shy of her 75th birthday while visiting at the Antlers hotel in Colorado Springs. Of her million dollar-plus estate, she left half to relatives, a quarter to her church, and, totally without warning, $350,000 to

Kansas City for the establishment of an art museum here.

For 16 years after her bombshell bequest, the city pondered how to use it in accordance with her will. By 1927 her gift had more than doubled in value. By happy coincidence, when William Rockhill Nelson died leaving his wealth for the purchase of works of art, and his heirs, earmarking their estates for a building to house such, the perfect solution was provided: combine Mary Atkins' bequest with the Nelson money for the creation of the Nelson Gallery of Art and Atkins Museum.

Thus did the enigmatic "lady in black" who lived the last five years of her modest life at the Washington hotel downtown, join with Baron Nelson and his millions to push Kansas City one step along the path toward culture.

# H. Roe Bartle

*c.1896-1974*

## Boy Scout Chief & Mayor

It's hard to imagine the monumental, outgoing Harold Roe Bennett Sturdevant Bartle being a vain man, but how else can one explain his keeping the year of his birth a secret?

Bartle was born in Richmond, Virginia on June 25, presumably 1896. He died in his adopted Kansas City 77 years later, give or take. The intervening years he filled with Scouting, eating, public speaking, banking and mayoring.

A living legend, Roe Bartle was many things by design, but a public speaker almost by default. Once upon a time that vast man with the volcanic voice was shy. To overcome it, as a schoolboy he was forced to stand and face his peers, speechifying. After two spectacular failures and one total retreat, he championed fear and took to public speaking with a vengeance, ultimately converting his new-found talent into a lucrative livelihood. Before long, H. Roe Bartle had become a glib, sonorous, compelling speaker, much in demand, and highly compensated.

Bartle, who came to Kansas City in 1928 while still in his early thirties, was a many-faceted man. Professional Scouting was the love of his life. Weighing 350 pounds at his apogee, 6′ 3″ Bartle in his tent-like hiking shorts was affectionately dubbed the Biggest Boy Scout of All.

As a serious, hard-working organizer, his board memberships were legion (17 at one count). As educator he once served as both president and chairman (unpaid) of Missouri Valley College in Marshall, Missouri. As farmer-stockman he operated spreads in both Missouri and Oklahoma. In Kansas City, his pet project, a training ground for youth leadership people, American Humanics Foundation, came to fruition under his tutelage. On top of all else, he was a lawyer who became mayor of Kansas City.

Cigar-chomping Bartle with booming voice, impressive height, vast girth and high visibility was elected Mayor in 1955 and re-elected four years later. During his reign his negotiations with Lamar Hunt lead to the Chiefs' move here from Dallas. In fact, Bartle became Mayor on the same day the Detroit Tigers arrived here to celebrate Kansas City's inauguration into big league football, April 11, 1955.

As Kansas City slipped into the sixties, H. Roe Bartle slipped out of mayoring, and back into his ancillary roles in Scouting and public speaking for his last 11 years. He died May 9, 1974, never revealing his exact age, estimated at almost 78. Posthumously, giant-sized Bartle Convention Hall was built downtown, memorializing Kansas City's larger-than-life former mayor.

21

# Thomas Hart Benton

*1889-1975*

Artist

**B**y some great good stroke of luck, Thomas Hart Benton, Missouri's artist laureate, died as he lived—brush in hand—just three months shy of his 86th birthday. As the sturdy, stubby bear of a man sat studying his just-completed mural for Nashville's Country Music Foundation Museum, he tumbled lifeless from his studio chair.

Tom Benton's legendary life began on April 15, 1889, in the southwest Missouri town of Neosho. Born into the illustrious clan which included Senator Thomas Hart Benton, the great-uncle whose name he bore, young Tom had a lot to live up to. His father, a Neosho lawyer, served as U.S. Representative from Missouri (1896-1904), and as U.S. Attorney under President Cleveland. Father Benton was as eloquent, highly individualistic, independent and strong-minded as his intractable son would become.

Young Tom, a contentious maverick who lived a Huck Finn-like childhood between small-town Missouri and big city Washington, D.C., showed a proclivity not for law but for drawing. His art, however, was just a hobby until he was 17 when a local barroom boast that he was "an artist" forced him to make good his words. Hiring on as staff artist with the nearby Joplin, Missouri AMERICAN, Tom outraged his father who whisked him off to military school. He lasted there long enough to quit and head for Chicago where, in 1907, he enrolled at age 18 in the Art Institute.

After Chicago Benton was off to Paris for three years, to New York for six, the Navy for one (where he was flyweight boxer, coal-shoveler and architectural draftsman.) Back in New York again, he resumed teaching at the Art Students League, married Rita Piacenza, one of his art students, and accepted commissions to paint murals—a genre that stood him in good stead until his death.

In the 1930s Tom Benton became the most important muralist in America, and in 1935 he returned to Kansas City to teach at the Kansas City Art Institute. Fortunately, a dispute with the school over morals, art and young minds led to his dismissal in 1941, which forced him into full-time painting. That was the beginning of his most productive and lucrative period. With canvases, murals and books, Benton made the big time.

The irascible artist and his wife of 53 years lived in casual comfort in a rambling three-story stone and shingle house at 3616 Belleview. There in his carriage house-studio out back, Thomas Hart Benton died on Sunday evening, January 19, 1975. Three months later, Rita followed. Their cremated remains were taken to their beloved Martha's Vineyard where they were buried in the wild garden of their summer home.

Now their Kansas City home and Benton's studio are open to the public as a house-museum.

23

# George Caleb Bingham

*1811-1879*

Painter

Mention Order No. 11, that infamous Civil War edict of depopulation hereabouts, and the name George Caleb Bingham springs to mind. Bingham, the bantam-sized, toupeed, fiery-tempered artist, vowed he would make the Order and General Thomas Ewing, who issued it, hated household words if it were imposed. It was, and he did.

Born on his family's tobacco plantation in Augusta County, Virginia, March 20, 1811, he was eight years old when the family "started anew" in Franklin, Missouri. Bingham's father died shortly thereafter, and at 16 George left home for nearby Boonville. There he apprenticed to a local artisan of speakerly persuasions who stirred both the young man's artistry and political curiosity.

Young Bingham's family moved to Arrow Rock then, where he grew up. That Bingham family home is now a house-museum. The young artist married there, and was sadly soon widowed. To assuage his grief and further refine his painting technique, he went east to study at the Pennsylvania Academy of Fine Arts. Returning, he pursued portrait painting with renewed vigor, his one-a-day output becoming legendary.

Long intrigued with political life, Bingham ran for public office (unsuccessfully) and served as State Treasurer (devotedly and well.) After marrying a second time, Bingham flirted with academia as superintendent of the art department at MU and art instructor at Stephens college, meanwhile painting large landscapes as well as his famous bread-and-butter portraits.

Bingham had moved to Independence prior to the Civil War when border incidents claiming innocent lives and property drove him to depictions of those local atrocities. His most famous was "Order No. 11", the graphic portrayal of Gen. Ewing imposing his dreaded order on Missouri-Kansas border residents. Bingham's Independence estate at 313 West Pacific street is now open as a house-museum.

Following the Civil War, Bingham moved to Kansas City where he was widowed a second time. His third wife was the widow of his friend and political ally Dr. Johnston Lykins. In 1874 Bingham, an ardent foe of "vice and dissipation", became President of the Police Board in wide open Kansas City, serving with fire and vigor. His final political appointment as State Adjutant General came the following year.

Bingham, genre painter, patriot, politician and public servant died in his 68th year on July 7, 1879. He lies in Union Cemetery with his third wife, and her first husband, Dr. Johnston Lykins, the three as close in death as they had been in life.

25

# Daniel Morgan Boone

*1769-1839*

Pioneer

Two days before Christmas 1769 Daniel Morgan Boone was born, the third son of that legendary frontiersman Daniel Boone of Kentucky. Since young Boone's two older brothers were killed by Indians, from his youth he was the eldest son. It is recorded that this son resembled his illustrious father, "a square little man with blue eyes and yellow hair, and a voice like a woman's." Their benign appearance belied the rugged frontier expolits of both.

According to some records, as early as 1787, almost 200 years ago, the sturdy 18 year old son came to mid-Missouri to hunt and trap beaver along the Big Blue River where he remained off and on for 25 years.

Daniel Morgan Boone's early education in Kentucky was as a surveyor which served him well throughout his lifetime. Trekking, trapping, hunting and exploring were all interlaced with surveying, stonemasonry and farming, at all of which he excelled.

In 1812 after his years along the Big Blue, Daniel Morgan became a captain in the war against England and did distinguished service in the west for the Union, retiring from the Army two years later. It was then the adventuresome Boones—Daniel Morgan, his brother Nathan, his sister Susannah and their growing families—headed west. Arriving in 1817, they were among the earliest settlers to come by wagon to Jackson County. And Daniel Morgan is generally credited with being the first white man to visit the site of Independence.

After several years as a government farmer to the Indians in Jefferson County, Kansas, Boone, his brother and sister and their bewildering array of offspring settled in Westport Township. Daniel Morgan's 1831 tract of 240 acres lay on the east side of what was to become the original Blue Hills Golf Course at 63rd street near Paseo.

There he lived out his last eight years farming and reminiscing a life of high adventure on the frontier. And there he died on June 13, 1839 at age 69 having sired a dozen children. He was laid to rest in a walnut coffin made by Henry Sager of Westport which cost $9.00. Following custom, Daniel Morgan Boone was buried on the home place in what came to be known as Boone-Hays cemetery near today's 63rd street and Brooklyn avenue.

Among the myriad and confusing Boone descendents was a son, Morgan, whose 1842 three-room log cabin with fireplace of "sawn stone" has been preserved by the Kansas City Museum. A nephew, Albert Gallatin Boone operated an outfitting store in the 1850s at 500 Westport road in the building that is now Kelly's Tavern.

JAMES BRIDGER
1804          1881

CELEBRATED AS A HUNTER, TRAPPER,
FUR TRADER AND GUIDE. DISCOVERED
GREAT SALT LAKE 1824. THE SOUTH
PASS 1827. VISITED YELLOWSTONE LAKE
AND GEYSERS 1830. FOUNDED FT. BRIDGER
1843. OPENED OVERLAND ROUTE BY
BRIDGER'S PASS TO GREAT SALT LAKE.
WAS GUIDE FOR U.S. EXPLORING
EXPEDITIONS ALBERT SIDNEY JOHNSTON'S
ARMY IN 1857, AND G.M. DODGE IN U.P.
SURVEYS AND INDIAN CAMPAIGNS 1865-66.
THIS MONUMENT IS ERECTED AS A
TRIBUTE TO HIS PIONEER WORK BY
MAJ. GEN. G.M. DODGE

# Jim Bridger

## *1804-1881*

## Mountain Man

Jim Bridger, a storybook frontiersman, was born in Virginia on St. Pat's Day, 1804. From 1824 until the late 1860s he was the premier Indian fighter, beaver trapper, fur trader, guide to the Wild West, storekeeper, scout, explorer, and discoverer. He was, in fact, about the most picturesque character in our western history. He also carried with him one large blot on his otherwise illustrious life.

In 1822 as an eager 18 year old, he was part of one of the most ignoble events on the frontier, the Hugh Glass affair. It was a sorry saga of a trapper badly mauled by a grizzly and being left to die by two impatient lads (taking the man's gun and ammunition and reporting his death and burial to their party leader) only to have what remained of old Hugh Glass catch up with them and "mete out a suitable punishment." Bridger was one of the two lads.

Perhaps this dishonorable episode sobered and chastened Jim Bridger who became a mountain man without peer, guiding more wagon trains than all other scouts put together on the westward trek. Bridger had an almost photographic memory for terrain, spoke not only English, French and Spanish, but six Indian tongues as well, and was chief of five Indian tribes to boot.

This incredible man with his incredible abilities became discoverer of the Great Salt Lake in 1824, of South Pass in 1827, of Yellowstone Park in 1830 (44 years before it was "officially" discovered), and founder of Fort Bridger on the Oregon Trail in 1843.

When the fur market in Europe crashed and ended his trapping career, Bridger switched to storekeeping, buying a general merchandise store which his son-in-law operated at 504 Westport road (site of today's Stanford and Sons restaurant.)

In 1855 he bought a farm near the old Dallas community south of Kansas City on State Line running from 103rd to 107th street and east to Wornall road. On the crest of the hill south of Indian Creek he built a stone farmhouse where he died, 77 and blind, on July 17,1881. He was buried about 200 yards northwest of 101st and Jefferson streets where he lay for almost 25 years.

In 1904 Maj. Gen. Grenville Dodge, the Union Pacific's engineer who had consulted with Bridger on the UP's route through the mountains, had the old explorer's remains moved. In gratitude for Bridger's advice which had made the UP first to the west, Gen. Dodge had an elaborate monument erected over Bridger's new resting place in Mt. Washington Cemetery.

# Thomas Bullene

*1828-1894*

## Merchant & Mayor

Thomas B. Bullene was to early Kansas City retailing what William Volker was to philanthropy or J. C. Nichols to real estate. He was tops.

Born in Oswego, New York in 1828, Bullene's business career began here in 1863. He was 35 when he and his brother Lathrop opened a small general merchandise store on the northwest corner of Missouri avenue and Main street. Twenty years later his Bullene Brothers and Emery retail establishment had become Kansas City's beloved behemoth, the late Emery, Bird, Thayer & Company department store. In 1890 this Number One retail establishment moved uptown to 11th street and Grand avenue, there to become a landmark and a legend.

Thomas B. Bullene was, from his arrival, part and parcel of Kansas City's civic, business and political life. His first year he became involved in the newly reorganized Board of Trade. Transportation would make or break his adopted city, he reasoned, and he set off for Washington, D. C. pleading for appropriations to improve navigation on the Missouri. Two years later his membership in the Board of Trade led to his lobbying on behalf of railroad lines here as well. He subsequently became president of the Kansas City Railroad Company, founder of the Kansas City Agricultural and Mechanical Association, director of the Merchants Exchange, and a member of the Board of Directors of the First National Bank. Thomas Bullene was a mover and a shaker.

He served as foreman of Kansas City's first fire company, first president of the Humane Society, and helped found the new Kansas City Club. With his ability for getting things done, in 1882 at the age of 54 Thomas B. Bullene was elected 22nd mayor of Kansas City.

During his tenure the first arc lights in the city were turned on. Another of his loves, fire-fighting, received world acclaim under his patronage when George C. Hale, Kansas City's exemplary fire chief, took his crack fire-fighting team to England to show their stuff.

Thomas B. Bullene's life ended in 1894 in Kansas City. In his 66 years he was master merchant, participating citizen and distinguished mayor. While the city's chief executive, Bullene's residence was downtown at 918 Baltimore avenue, the address of today's University Club.

# Col. Theodore S. Case

*1832-1900*

Soldier

Theodore Spencer Case was a genial doctor, born January 26, 1832 in Jackson, Georgia. He left his mark on Kansas City as an historian but preferred to be remembered as a soldier. He arrived here in 1857 at age 25. Among his myriad achievements was editing the town's first history—a street-by-street description which constitutes the city's first "business directory" and catalogs the city's growth with biographical sketches of early settlers as well.

Dr. Case, along with Kersey Coates, Robert Van Horn, Thomas Swope, John Calvin McCoy, William Gilliss and the various offspring of James Hyatt McGee, constituted Kansas City's pre-Civil War elite. They were the founders and shapers in our town. Unlike the others however, Case was never a man of money.

In 1851 after finishing school at Marietta College, Ohio, Theodore Case taught school and studied medicine. Two years later, a freshly graduated physician, he came to Kansas City, practicing here until the Civil War. This Georgia gentleman then enlisted in the Union Army, serving as Chief Quartermaster of the military district of this border area and of the state of Missouri. In 1861 he became a Second Lieutenant in Robert Van Horn's battalion, resigning to private life later with the rank of Colonel—a title he thereafter retained.

Case's journalistic reputation began with two papers he edited, the POST and FREE STATE REPUB-LICAN. Both ceased publication in 1861 in the maelstrom of Civil War sentiment. He again put pen to paper in the Army, writing and publishing the "Quartermasters Guide", the Bible of military procurement.

Always available for public service, Case was appointed railroad commissioner in 1866, and a University curator the following year. He was first president of the Real Estate and Stock Exchange, and with his brother, operated an agricultural implement manufacturing company. In 1870 he organized and was president of the Commerical Bank, and from 1873-1886 served as postmaster.

Col. Case, the lanky, bearded, blue-eyed optimist, died April 9, 1900 at age 68. His obituary describes an able, active, willing hand who "was a justice of the peace, a scientist, banker, literateur, businessman, professional man and public official." He lies in Elmwood Cemetery where the one-word entry on his burial card reads simply "soldier."

33

LEANNAH KEARNS
1843 — 1935

# Annie Chambers

*1843-1935*

## Madam

Leannah Loveall Chambers Kearns alias "Annie Chambers" was for fifty years Kansas City's most notorious madam. Her infamous "resort" was on the southwest corner of Third and Wyandotte streets, a block west of the present Victoria Station restaurant.

The innocent Annie was born June 6, 1843 near Lexington, Kentucky. She died 91 years later on March 24, 1935, woefully alone and nearly blind in her two-story red brick house near the riverfront.

Her route from Kentucky to Kansas City via Indianapolis, according to the legend that surrounds her, was strewn with pathos and tragedy. There was a too-severe father, a vanished husband, a dead child or two, general mistreatment at the hands of the world, and her ultimate resolution to fight back.

The professional Annie Chambers first cast her tall, large-boned shadow on Kansas City in 1869. An alert businesswoman, she quickly sized up a likely situation and in short order opened her first "house" here on the north side of the river. There beyond the long arm of the law, she plied her trade for three years. A flourishing ferry delivered her loyal following until she relocated in the town proper, at 3rd and Wyandotte streets in 1872. There for half a century she prospered, became a whispered household word, gaining her tainted reputation.

Apparently her rapport with the law enabled her, with occasional periods of down-time, to continue with impunity until 1923. After that, the aging Annie went straight, operating her establishment as a garden-variety boarding house, with clientele largely limited to railroad men.

During the final decade of her life, Annie was befriended by the benevolent Reverend Bulkley and his wife who owned adjoining property where they operated the City Mission. It was their kind ministrations which saw her through a pitiful decline and ultimate passing, and arranged her funeral and burial at Elmwood. In return, Kansas City's most talked-about madam left her house to the Bulkleys for their City Mission, ironically a refuge for fallen men.

35

CHICK

Col. WILLIAM MILES CHICK
1794 — 1847
FIRST SETTLER AND FIRST POST MASTER
OF KANSAS CITY MISSOURI
AND
HIS BELOVED WIFE
ANN ELIZA SMITH
1796 — 1876

# Col. William Miles Chick

*1794-1847*

## Town Father

Virginia-born William Miles Chick came to Westport in 1836 from Alexandria, Virginia by way of Glasgow, Missouri. He was 42 when he arrived here and opened a store with Westport founder John Calvin McCoy. Chick shortly helped form the Town Company of Kansas and became known as its "first citizen" who lavished his easy Virginia hospitality on all "principal visitors."

From the outset Chick was a VIP acting as one of the three commissioners charged with deciding the disposition of the late Gabriel Prudhomme's estate, clearing the legal path for establishment of today's Kansas City.

Between 1843 and 1844 Chick built a long, two-story, boarded log structure with massive stone chimneys at both ends. It was a frontier mansion perched atop a hill overlooking the river landing at Walnut street between 2nd and Pearl streets.

He built one of the first businesses here, a storage and commission house consisting of two log rooms 20 feet apart. Located on high ground near the levee at the southeast corner of Main street, it miraculously survived the flood of 1844. Another of Chick's waterfront ventures was a bustling ferry service which he operated between his place of business and the north bank of the Missouri.

In 1845 William Miles Chick was appointed first postmaster, and among his other milestones he is credited with persuading Bent and St. Vrain to operate their freighting business from the Town of Kansas in 1845. By offering them warehousing facilities, Chick was able to divert the rich Santa Fe trade here.

Col. Chick and his wife, Ann Eliza Smith Chick, produced five sons, all of whom were educated at the Shawnee Indian Mission, and five daughters, all of whom married well (becoming brides of John Calvin McCoy, Nathan Scarritt, William Johnson, Thompson Peery, and John W. Polk.) Chick was a Virginian who fought in the War of 1812, and a quarter of a century later helped found our new town on the frontier.

He died at age 53 on April 7, 1847. His was the second burial in the then new public Town Cemetery at 5th and Oak streets. Now he lies in Union Cemetery, land forming a "union" between the old town of Westport and the new Town of Kansas, both of which he served.

ERECTED TO THE MEMORY OF
BRIGITTE
WIFE OF
R. H. DUTHAU Sr. Jr.
BORN JUNE 9, 1778.
DIED MAY 18, 1829.
CONSORT OF
FRANCES CHOUTEAU
BORN FEB. 7, 1767
DIED APR. 18, 1858

# Bereniece and Francois Chouteau

*1801-1888*        *1797-1838*

## First White Settlers

When Bereniece and Francois Chouteau, high-bred French newlyweds, arrived from St. Louis in 1821 they were the area's first white settlers. She was a teen-age bride and had just celebrated her 20th birthday. He was 24.

Bereniece Chouteau was the daughter of Col. Pierre Menard, first Lt. Governor of Illinois, whose handsomely restored French Colonial home of 1802 is open to the public at Fort Kaskaskia State Park in southwest Illinios.

Francois was the son of Pierre Chouteau, a prominent St. Louisan, and a nephew of Auguste, the man who had founded and planned the building of our sister city to the east. It was Auguste Chouteau who first sent his young nephew west in 1819-20 looking for warehouse sites for the family's ever-expanding fur interests.

The following year Francois Chouteau returned here accompanied by his rich, cultured, musically-talented, convent-educated French wife. For her he built their first home on the river, a few miles east of today's downtown. In 1826, both it and the first Chouteau warehouse were flooded out. They resettled in a house on the river bluff near the foot of Troost and Forest avenues, there to raise their ten children, nine sons and one daughter.

A second Chouteau fur warehouse was rebuilt on higher ground too, in what became Guinotte's Addition, and there it flourished from 1826 until 1844 when it was flooded again and abandoned.

Francois died in 1838 at age 41. He was buried in the old Catholic burying ground in downtown St. Louis, and moved to the Calvary cemetery family plot at mid-century. Madame Chouteau lived another 50 years, becoming Kansas City's real pioneer mother, raising their ten children and finding time "to mother most of the rest of the community as well."

When she died at 87 in 1888, Madame Chouteau had out-lived her husband, all her children, and most of her friends—the McCoys, the Chicks, and the Troosts.

KERSEY COATE

# Kersey Coates

*1823-1887*

## Quality Hill

Kersey Coates, a man of slight build and elegant manner, was a Kansas City giant. From the year of his arrival, Coates was leader of the young town's influential Northern commercial element—in building, banking, investing and in merchandising (with Thomas Bullene in the forerunner of Emery, Bird, Thayer & Company.) Everything he did, everything he touched exuded style and quality. In fact, "Quality" might well have been his middle name. Where Kansas City was concerned, he never compromised.

Kersey Coates was born September 15, 1823 to a wealthy Pennsylvania Quaker family, and after a proper schooling, he practiced law with that radical Pennsylvania Republican Thaddeus Stevens. Coates came to Kansas City for the first time in 1854 representing a group of Philadelphia capitalists who had money to invest in the west. Once here, however, Coates was consumed with the promise in this young town, returning east only long enough to borrow funds to establish himself here, and to collect his young bride.

Settling here in the spring of 1856, by November he was a director of the recently organized Kansas City, Hannibal and St. Joseph Railroad Company, and a partner in one of the town's first banking establishments, Coates & Hood. As Coates & Company he began investing in real estate on the city's West Side bluffs where his attractive neighborhood soon became the most fashionable residential address in town—dubbed

Quality Hill. And there he built his own handsome two and one-half story red brick house at the southwest corner of 10th street and Pennsylvania avenue (named after his native state), on a homesite he purchased from the widow Bereniece Chouteau.

The following year Coates was an incorporating member of the Chamber of Commerce. When Civil War seemed imminent, the rock-ribbed Republican and staunch Unionist joined the battalion of his fellow Pennsylvanian, newspaperman Robert T. Van Horn. Ironically, the foundation of what was to become his Coates House hotel stabled the horses of his Union forces.

Following the war years, Coates and his former commanding officer, Congressman Robert T. Van Horn and Charles E. Kearney brought the railroads to Kansas City. It was that signal event which led to construction of the Hannibal Bridge in 1869, making Kansas City the transportation gateway to the west.

Kersey Coates died April 24, 1887 at age 63, still the gentlest of men, leaving an estate of two million dollars.

# Bernard Corrigan

*1847-1914*

## Street Railway

**B**ernard Corrigan's name conjures up two things: Kansas City's first citywide street railway, and one of the most spectacular houses in the Country Club district.

"Barney" Corrigan, as he was always known, was born in Quebec August 15, 1847 to a successful Canadian farm family. Twenty-one years later he and three brothers came to Kansas City to make their mark. When he died here 46 years later, Corrigan had made his fortune, largely in railroads, but for the most part other than in Kansas City. He always said he made his money elsewhere, but spent it here.

Corrigan's wealth came from building giant railroads like the Denver & Rio Grande, Oregon Short Line, and Kansas City Southern, and from constructing enormous power dams and viaducts, largely in Texas. With this largesse, Barney Corrigan and his older brother Thomas bought up their competition here, pulling together 15 rail lines of every type, and creating one single city-wide streetcar system for Kansas City that really worked. A first for our town before 1900.

In 1902 Barney Corrigan became president of the Metropolitan Railway Company and of the Kansas City Electric Light Company as well.

Barney Corrigan's more popular renown stems from the house he was building in 1914. He and brother Thomas and their respective large families lived in matching mansions, shoulder-to-shoulder at 17th and Summit streets. In 1912 Barney commissioned Kansas City's flamboyant architect and fellow Canadian Louis Curtiss to design a splendid, if somewhat "smaller", house (of 25 rooms) for his gradually diminishing family. Corrigan had sired 18 offspring: ten by his first wife, and eight by his second. Of his 14 living children, several had already de-camped and others were soon to follow.

Curtiss designed a strikingly modern horizontal two-story Art Nouveau house of concrete construction faced with Carthage cut stone for the large corner lot on the northwest corner of 55th and Ward Parkway. With copious stained glass windows and a wide overhanging roofline, it was estimated to cost upwards of $200,000 by the projected March 1, 1914 move-in date.

But on January 6, only a few minutes before going south to inspect its progress, 66 year old Barney Corrigan was stricken and died. Sadly, the Corrigans never occupied their stunning house, still much admired at 1200 West 55th street.

# Asa Beebe Cross

*1826-1894*

Architect

Kansas City's first "name" architect was Asa Beebe Cross. He came to this frontier place in 1857 when he was not yet 30.

Cross was born in Tuckahoe, New Jersey December 9, 1826, and before he was 20 had sailed around the world twice on ships belonging to his uncle. On one wild voyage he was shipwrecked off the coast of Patagonia for six weeks before rescue. Fortunately for Kansas City, he *was* rescued.

Back on dry land Cross studied architecture in the 1850s first in Philadelpia and then in St. Louis. There he became a partner with his architecture professor; worked briefly in St. Paul; returned to St. Louis long enough to marry; and came to Kansas City, as a lumber dealer-architect.

Asa Beebe Cross lived, worked and practiced his considerable talent here for 36 years, leaving a monumental mark—Vaughan's Diamond at the Junction of 9th and Main streets; the Keith & Perry Building at 9th and Grand avenue; the second Jackson County Courthouse; the first Union Depot in the West Bottoms; the Gilliss Opera House and bank building at 5th and Delaware streets—all gone now except in photos.

Of his "survivors" are old St. Patrick's Cathedral at 800 Cherry street with twin belfries and symmetrical Italianate Revival styling, and down in the River Quay area, two of his commercial buildings: the old Board of Trade at 502 Delaware street, now much altered; and Pacific House hotel at 401 Delaware street with a gracefully arched ironwork facade. It was here Civil War Gen. Thomas Ewing was headquartered and issued his infamous Order No. 11.

Out south, the 1871-2 remodeling and enlargement of Seth Ward's fine Greek Revival-style farmhouse at 1032 West 55th street is Cross' elegant handiwork. In Independence, Cross designed the Harvey Vaile mansion ten years later, an imposing 30-room Victorian pile of red brick and cut stone replete with fancy-work wood trim painted white, patterned multi-colored slate roof and towering four-story cupola.

Sixty-seven year old Asa Beebe Cross died August 18, 1894 as his remodeling of the old Clay County Courthouse in Liberty neared completion. Sadly, it's gone too, but we're richer by far to have even a sprinkling of his splendid survivors.

45

# Louis Curtiss

*1865-1924*

## Architect

Louis Singleton Curtiss, although "very short and a little wide", was actually larger-than-life. His personal flamboyance might have obscured his genius had the latter not been so real and enduring. Canadian by birth and an eccentric bachelor by choice, the architect lived in Kansas City from the late 1880s until his death at age 58 in 1924.

Louis Curtiss was born July 1, 1865 in Belleville, Canada, studied architecture at the University of Toronto and in Paris before coming to Kansas City. Here he joined another talented 25 year old, Frederick C. Gunn in a partnership which produced gems like the Missouri State Building for the 1893 World's Columbian Exposition in Chicago, and the quaintly eclectic chapel at the Veterans Hospital in Leavenworth, Kansas, as well as the Tarrant County Court House in Fort Worth.

When his partnership dissolved, the enormously gifted, and by then well-heeled Louis Curtiss set off on his own, living an intoxicating existence, smoking monogrammed Turkish cigarettes, wearing a wardrobe of white, and driving (very fast) one of the first automobiles in Kansas City. Dramatic to the nth degree, he consulted with the spirit world, paid his rent in gold coin, and cut his own hair.

But Louis Curtiss was no mere dilettante, as his remarkable and disparate designs testify.

Witness his Folly Theatre on the northwest corner of 12th and Central streets, recently restored and reopened.

In 1908 Curtiss built two flagship designs here—the Boley Clothing Company building on the northwest corner of 12th and Walnut streets, and the three-story concrete-framed Curtiss Studio building at 1118 McGee street. The latter contained stores on the ground floor; his office and drafting room on the second; and on the third, Curtiss' unique and exotic living quarters with a rooftop courtyard opening off his bedroom which "surveyed the city through walls of floor-to-ceiling glass."

After designing the Baltimore hotel for the Corrigan Realty Company in 1898, Bernard Corrigan became the architect's great patron. In 1912 Curtiss designed Corrigan's contemporary all-concrete house at 55th and Ward Parkway. With Corrigan's sudden death in 1914 Curtiss lost his angel, and his practice ground to a halt.

Louis Curtiss, withdrawn and introspective, was sitting at the drawing board in his studio when he died on June 24, 1924, a week short of his 59th birthday. Not surprisingly, this totally unorthodox man requested burial in an unmarked grave.

LUCY CHRISTIE
DRAGE
SEPT. 18, 1876
SEPT. 11, 1965

# Lucy Drage

*1876-1965*

## Interior Decorator

**B**ack in the years when she was operating her business, from 1930 to 1965, Lucy Drage, who decorated interiors, was called an Interior Decorator. And everything she did was done to that certain Drage style.

Born Lucy Christie September 18, 1876, the daughter of wealthy Kansas City grain broker C. C. Christie, she grew up on Quality Hill in the era when that West Bluff neighborhood was quite an elegant showplace. In her 88 jam-packed years, Mrs. Drage became an artist and interior decorator; traveler and lecturer; wife and mother; business manager of her father's Christie Farms; co-founder of the National Bundles-for-Britain relief program; and a Fellow in the AID.

Even her marriage bore her certain style. Lucy Christie married an Englishman, Francis B. Drage who, at the time of their meeting, was a Colonel in the Royal Horse Guards, escorts of the British monarch no less. Afterwards they lived in England for ten years, on the Drage estate near Northampton. Later they made their home here at "Stony Glen", what was then a fine stone and frame mansion at 7607 Indiana; now a vacant field on a dead-end street east of decaying Fairyland Park.

As a young lady with artistic talent, Lucy began taking painting lessons at the Kansas City Art Institute the first year it opened downtown. She continued studying until the year she died, becoming a lifelong benefactor, and founding member of the Institute's Fireside Committee—a support group renowned for its Sunday suppers and fund-raising prowess into the 1950s. For years Lucy Drage and ten fellow painters shared studio space at 45th street and State Line road, an area recently revived as an arts and antiques Mecca.

It was after her marriage and ten years' residence in England and rearing three children that the energetic lady began casting about for a career. She and the late Ethel Guy decided to become partners in Lucy Drage Interior Decorating Inc., a firm of the first water. The company became a venerated fixture at 320 Ward Parkway, from which studio they decorated the town's biggest and the best for 35 years, including the then-new Kansas City Country Club.

Colonel Drage died in 1935 in his native England. Thirty years later the doyenne herself died September 11, 1965 just one week before her 89th birthday. Lucy Drage Interior Decorating Inc. closed its doors and an era ended.

49

# Elizabeth and U. S. Epperson

*1855-1939*        *1861-1927*

## Philanthropists

Uriah Spray Epperson was born in Indiana December 22, 1861, and came to Kansas City when he was eight. He died 65 years later having made a large fortune for himself, raised a small fortune for charity, and provided amply for his widow to do likewise.

Elizabeth Weaver Epperson never told a soul the date of her birth, which was March 25, 1855. She died October 22, 1939, and guarded guesses were that she was over 75. Actually she was almost 85. In her widowhood Mrs. Epperson became an unobtrusive and gracious giver. The Eppersons had shared an interest in fine arts. He was a painter who never took time to develop his talents; both loved music.

From 1890 until 1902 while young Epperson was General Manager of the Fowler Meat Packing interests, he fell in with a philanthropic scheme to raise money for worthy causes, and have fun at the same time. His friend William Rockhill Nelson dreamed up the idea of a minstrel group which would strut for charity. Nelson would sponsor the first production if Epperson would organize, drill and lead the troop.

Epperson, a Music Man at heart, was easily convinced, and the Epperson Megaphone Mastodon Minstrels were born. One hundred twenty-five finely-tuned, black-faced, top-hatted performers with swinging canes and matching megaphones, marched, played, danced and joked

their way into the pocketbooks of Kansas Citians, raising $85,000 for city betterment.

In 1902 U. S. Epperson organized the Epperson Land & Investment Company and later, the U. S. Epperson Underwriting Company. His business prospered and the insurance executive and his wife built a monumental home at 5200 Cherry street, a grand Tudor-Gothic castle complete with mezzanine for string orchestra.

When Mr. Epperson died just four years later, Mrs. Epperson blossomed into a patroness of the arts. In his memory she built U. S. Epperson Hall at the Kansas City Art Institute, gave the Conservatory of Music practice instruments and a library of musical scores, and did the same for the fledgling Philharmonic. Until she became house-bound in 1938, Mrs. Epperson never missed a Philharmonic concert, and when she could no longer attend, Conductor Karl Krueger and 40 players performed for her in her baronial castle on one occasion.

After a year's illness, Mrs. Epperson died leaving her house to KCU (now UMKC class-rooms), $15,000 to the Philharmonic, $50,000 to the Art Institute, and her cherished collection of 100 antique theatre handbills to the city!

51

# Myrtle and Charles Fillmore

*1845-1931      1854-1948*

Unity School

Unity School of Christianity was founded by Charles and Myrtle Fillmore who got there by dint of hard work. In the late 1880s the Fillmores were down and almost out when they gave birth to the idea that became Unity.

Charles Fillmore was born August 22, 1854 on an Indian reservation near St. Cloud, Minnesota where his father was a Chippewa trader. Myrtle Fillmore was born in Pagetown, Ohio, nine years earlier on October 6, 1845. They met in Texas; he, a railroad freight clerk suffering from tuberculosis; she, a school teacher in fragile health. They married, had two frail sons, and roamed the west seeking a cure.

In 1884 the Fillmores came to Kansas City which was in the midst of a building boom. They invested what they had in real estate, and lost. Picking up the pieces they made a decision: spiritual work would be their future. Myrtle had been much impressed by Emma Curtis Hopkins, a pioneer in the New Thought movement in the west. Charlie was an articulate and persuasive man of deep beliefs. Together they launched Unity School of Christianity in 1889.

Neither church nor sect, Unity leaned heavily on the written word, their printed pieces selling at cost for "love offerings." They started small, printing MODERN THOUGHT magazine. By 1906 Unity had a real publishing plant and an expanding repertoire. In 1920 they moved into their own building, offering food for the body as well as for the soul at 913 Tracy, preaching, printing and broadcasting, combined with a legendary Unity Inn serving vegetarian meals. From there emanated SILENT UNITY and radio station WOQ; WEE WISDOM for kiddies and DAILY WORD for adults.

In 1927 Unity moved to 1300 rolling acres at Bannister road and 50 highway in a self-contained village. Son Rick, a landscape designer and architect, unleashed his ingenuity and deft touch on the complex of Spanish Revival buildings which house Unity's world headquarters. Built of warm pinkish beige "antiqued" stucco and roofed with rosy tiles, it clusters around the landmark Unity Tower, giving onto a fountain running lengthwise of the manicured grounds. Midway is the Bridge of Faith, site of weddings, concerts and outdoor functions.

Eighty-six year old Myrtle Fillmore died October 6, 1931. Charlie Fillmore remarried and remained an active Unity force until his death at age 93 on July 5, 1948 when the ashes of both founders were reportedly scattered from the Bridge into the waters below.

JOHN BAILEY GAGE
FEBRUARY 24, 1887
JANUARY 15, 1970

# John B. Gage

*1887-1970*

## Clean-up Mayor

John Bailey "Jack" Gage and his clean-up campaign of the late 1930s spelled doom for Kansas City machine politics. Gage was a straight-shooter. A single-mindedly honest man, the lawyer son of a lawyer father. Born of early Kansas City stock, he grew up living history, and ended up making it.

Gages have figured prominently in political affairs here since Civil War times—the father's law firm dating from 1859 with the senior Gage serving as city attorney during that war, and later as Missouri legislator. Son John B. (or Jack to his intimates) was born February 24, 1887 on the family's 80-acre farm near 9th and Cleveland.

Jack Gage was a stem-winder. He went to the University of Kansas and debated; attended Kansas City School of Law, teaching nights and working days in his father's law firm. Not content to ride his father's broad coattails, son Jack started his own firm, which still bears his name today.

His personally unpretentious manner ("with his cackling laugh he could be downright folksy") belied the fire and drive beneath his surface. A non-partisan form of city government was the passion of his life. At 52, Jack Gage was reluctant to run for mayor, but once committed, he was a tiger. On the podium he was a slashing, hammering campaigner speaking always as a "nonpartisan candidate", labeling City Hall politics as "punishable law violations." And he meant it. He promised to give decent laws back to decent citizens and he meant that too. Naturally, he won.

It was Kansas City's good fortune to have John B. Gage for mayor not once, but three times, from 1940-1946. He got L. P. Cookingham for city manager, and together they brought in the charter amendments for a real merit system (exams for all city employees), and instituted non-partisan government with no monkey business.

In his first whirlwind year he cut the city budget $700,000 and set up businesslike procedures for the virtually bankrupt city he had inherited. After six years of Gage rule, Kansas City was $20,000,000 better off than the day he took office.

To Kansas Citians who remember the dirty thirties, the 1940 clean-up campaign (billed as the "Battle of the Brooms") and the name John B. Gage evoke one thing: honesty. He saved the city from itself. When he died at 82 on January 15, 1970, the aftermath of being struck while crossing 11th and Grand on his way to work, Kansas City lost its personality of the 40s—Mr. Nice-and-Clean.

55

# William Gilliss

*c.1797-1869*

Founder

William Gilliss (spelled then with two "s"s) was born in Somerset County, Maryland about 1797. He arrived here in 1831, having lived a roistering 34 years. He ran away to sea at age 14, served in General William Henry Harrison's Indian campaigns, built houses in Cincinnati, and traded profitably with the Delawares in Illinois. There he married a Delaware woman, had a child or two, then decamped.

Gilliss came here a "bachelor", living in solitary splendor. He built a land empire on bargain basement real estate. In 1832 he patented 228 acres on the west bluff at 26th street and State Line. There looking down on the main Shawnee trail (Southwest boulevard), he built his prosperous trading post. Within four years he owned much of today's West Side, south to Coleman Highlands.

In 1838 when the first public sale of Gabriel Prudhomme's farm to 14 shareholders was held, William Gilliss, who signed himself "gentleman", bought one share. At the court-ordered second sale ten years later, he bought three, and in time became one of the largest holders in the original Town.

In 1849 with Dr. Benoist Troost, husband of his favorite niece Mary, he built Gilliss House, the town's first hotel on Front street between Wyandotte and Delaware. A backer of the town's first newspaper, he was also an incorporator of the Chamber of Commerce, promoter of railroads, and together with Kersey Coates owned a general store which gave birth, ultimately, to Emery, Bird, Thayer & Company.

Wealthy William Gilliss built himself a tenroom southern colonial mansion at 2727 Holly on his one square mile farm (from Summit to State Line; from 23rd street to the Westport city limit.) Typically his was a two-story galleried brick house with ell. Atypically, it was covered with bright white sandstone plaster tooled to resemble cut stone which "sparkled like marble after the rain." Inside were stained glass windows, marble mantels and solid black walnut woodwork.

Inevitably he was raided by Kansas redlegs, banned by Gen. Ewing's Order No. 11, and returned after the edict to live out his days at 4th and Locust streets, still the wealthiest man in town. He died at age 72 on July 18, 1869 and lies in Union Cemetery, one of four of our Town founders buried there.

His name still lives on, both with one and with two "s"s. His devoted niece Mary Troost established the Gilliss Orphans' Home, now the Gillis Home for Children, as a memorial to the parsimonious "bachelor" who ironically had abandoned his own half-breed children 40 years earlier.

# Robert C. Greenlease, Sr.

*1882-1969*

## Cadillac Dealer

The middle initial in Robert C. Greenlease's name might have stood for "Cadillac", so closely were the two connected. By coincidence both the man and the car began business in 1903. But not together. Not for five years did they join forces.

Robert Greenlease was born a farmboy on August 25, 1882 near Slater, Missouri. His father was a horse-breeder who managed to do poorly enough that after several years of augmenting the family coffers holding public office, he moved his family to Kansas City and, hopefully, to greener pastures.

Here the young son attended Webster school until sixth grade, quit to work as office boy at Swift and Company packing plant, and there in 1894 saw his first horseless carriage—a red, high-wheeled affair with linen encased driver, lofty behind the wheel. Robert Greenlease was smitten for life.

After three years at Swift, his Uncle George, who headed Weber Gas Engine Company, hired the teen-ager and exposed him to a kindred soul— a natural tinkerer and former jewelryman named appropriately Pearl Karshner. In six years' time the two formed a partnership to manufacture an automobile they called the "Hummer."

Robert Greenlease was 21. The year was 1903—a banner year for cars. In Detroit Henry Ford was getting in gear; Henry Leland's Cadillac made its appearance; and in Kansas City the Hummer began (and ended) production, with one car.

In 1905 young Greenlease opened Central Automobile and Livery Company which grew steadily from one single-cylinder Cadillac to seven in two years' time. Next, Greenlease tried selling Thomas Flyers—a seven-passenger car with double chain drive—but it was a big car, unfortunately, when buyers were thinking small. So enterprising Greenlease went after the little four-cylinder Cadillac.

In 1908 he was able to buy eight, year-old Caddies at a markdown, and they sold like hotcakes. Greenlease and Cadillac had met and married. The car was five years old then, and not yet a part of General Motors. The man was 26 and on the road to becoming the largest and ultimately the last of GM's dealer-distributors. Along the way he became a multi-millionaire, and his name, synonymous with Cadillac in six states.

Sixty years later on September 17, 1969, 87 year old Robert Greenlease died, and a vintage chapter in automobile history was *fini*.

# Joseph Guinotte

*1815-1867*

## Early Civilizer

Joseph Guinotte was a civil engineer who came to America via northern France and Mexico. Born in Liege, Belgium, he was sent to Mexico in the 1840s by the Belgian government to supervise railroad construction. When war broke out between Mexico and the United States, the project was abandoned and Guinotte headed north, then down the Missouri river to what was known as Westport Landing.

The young bachelor arrived here in 1848 just as the Town of Kansas was being organized. Acting as an agent for the Belgian government he bought 1200 acres of the rich flatland of the East Bottoms from the widow of Francois Chouteau. Then he brought Belgian colonists to settle and develop it. Accomplished gardeners, they soon turned those acres into the town's market basket and beauty spot.

Guinotte also bought from Mme. Chouteau, a friend and fellow European emigre, her large log house which perched on a high bluff between 3rd and 4th streets, Troost to Lydia, at the site of today's Guinotte Manor. Two years later, in 1852, Guinotte sent to Brussels for his fiancee, the dainty, proper, French-speaking Aimee Brichaut. In New York he met her boat, they married in the first St. Patrick's Cathedral there, and came to this faraway place to make their home.

On the site of Mme. Chouteau's log house overlooking the East Bottoms and the Belgian community below, the young couple built a fine southern-style mansion. There Aimee Guinotte maintained a hospitable and cultured homelife despite the roughneck atmosphere of the surroundings. Among the Guinotte's many civilizing touches here, she brought one of the first pianos to Kansas City. And Joseph Guinotte, a great lover of flowers, imported the first dahlia tubers to Kansas City from Belgium. In this outback of the mid-1800s, small items of taste and beauty counted for much, as the Guinottes proved.

Joseph Guinotte was only 52 when he died in 1867. He was buried in the old Catholic cemetery downtown and moved in 1881 to Mt. St. Mary's cemetery. Twenty-two years later, Aimee Brichaut Guinotte, still tenaciously French-speaking, died and was laid to rest beside him.

# Joyce C. Hall

*1891-1982*

## Hallmark Cards

Joyce C. Hall, youthful picture-postcard peddler cum merchant prince of the greeting card world, started small while thinking big. Born August 29, 1891 in the barely-there Nebraska town of David City (although Norfolk claims him), he lived most of his long and productive life here.

At age 18 the lanky six-footer hit Kansas City selling scenic postal cards. Liking the prospects here, he stayed to prosper. What happened wasn't overnight, but he founded Hall Brothers which became Hallmark Cards Incorporated—the huge home-grown family-owned fun-factory producing greeting cards and much more.

The quiet, serious, highly sensitive young Joyce Hall went from jobbing postcards as a teen-ager to manufacturing and selling his own line in six years. World War I created a market for cards expressing sentimental thoughts to "the boys over there", and Hall's greeting card business took off.

The rest is an old-fashioned up-by-the-boot-straps success story with Hallmark leading the pack in the cheer-industry today. By how much is anybody's guess since seventy-five percent of its stock was family held at Hall's death in 1982. When he died his 72 year old, billion-dollar company had garnered its fame from many quarters: from "caring enough to send the very best" in cards and from long-lived sponsorship of quality television ("Hallmark Hall of Fame"); from major support in founding "People to People"(a

sort of private Peace Corps) and from Hall's lavish real estate venture at Crown Center. With Hall-mark's international headquarters at 25th street and McGee trafficway, their mid-town hotel/office/retail/residential project encompasses all things tony and tasteful in an initially $350 million urban redevelopment project.

Most of the Joyce Hall rags-to-riches story is boringly familiar. But one aspect rarely broached is the founder's unusual given name. "Joyce" apparently plagued him into adulthood and even after he had achieved some degree of fame. It had, he explained, derived from the surname of an admired Methodist bishop, Isaac W. Joyce of Minneapolis. And although a bit of a burden to him, he admitted never seriously considering using his middle name in its stead. "Clyde", as he pointed out, "wasn't any great shakes of a name either." Hence to his associates, he was simply "Mr. J. C."

Joyce Hall died at age 91 on October 29, 1982, leaving Kansas City a legacy of the highest quality.

# Hare & Hare

*1860-1938          1888-1960*

## Landscape Architects

Hare and Hare, father and son, were the first and last word in Kansas City landscape architecture from the late teens into the 1930s. Any large and prestigious project from that era bears witness. Downtown the Courthouse, City Hall and Municipal Courts complex is theirs; the Nelson-Atkins Museum of Art; J. C. Nichols' vast Country Club empire; and parks and cemeteries on both sides of the state line. And scores of cities in 28 states owe their ambiance to Hare and Hare, including R. A. Long's planned city of Longview, Washington.

Father and guiding light was Sid J. Hare, a gentle, scholarly, investigative man. He was born January 26, 1860 in Louisville, Kentucky, and came to Kansas City eight years later. Trained as a surveyor and civil engineer, his first love remained horticulture.

In 1896 these two melded when Sid Hare was appointed superintendent of Forest Hill cemetery. There for six years he lovingly sculpted the terrain's rolling contours, designed curving roadways, laid native stone walls and planted hundreds of varieties of trees—making Forest Hill "more than just a monument field."

Sid Hare had more sides than a diamond. From engineer to horticulturalist to amateur geologist was no stretch for his fertile imagination. For years he painstakingly unearthed, identified and catalogued upwards of 500 fossil remains from Kansas City building sites. And he also found time to be an avid armchair Egyptologist—working on the theory that within the Great Pyramid's Secret Chamber would be found the Ark of the Covenant, the Golden Candlesticks and other sacred utensils.

In 1902 Sid Hare started his own consulting firm, and eight years later, he was joined by his son, S. Herbert, a landscape architect who had studied under Frederick Law Olmstead at Harvard. Thus Hare and Hare was born in 1910.

When Sid Hare moved to his country place in 1924, "Harecliff", this 21-acre tract of wooded valley on Gregory boulevard near Blue Ridge, became his hobby. There he cultivated every weed and wild flower indigenous to Missouri. The Santa Fe Trail had passed across this refuge, and Cave Spring where pioneers had refreshed themselves and their livestock lay just beyond. Hare venerated the history as much as the land.

Sid Hare was 78 when he died at Harecliff October 25, 1938. He came full circle. His deft touch began at Forest Hill cemetery. Now he and his partner-son, who died in 1960, lie buried there, not far from the site of the house occupied at 69th street and Troost avenue during Sid Hare's cemetery superintendency.

65

# Col. John Harris

## 1798-1874
## Hotelkeeper

Mention John Harris' name and you may get blank stares. Mention Harris House, and you'll get confusion. This early Westport settler, his long-gone Harris House hotel, and his still-extant two-story red brick home are hard for most people to sort out.

John Harris was born December 4, 1798 in Madison County, Kentucky. He and his wife and the first six of their eight children came here by covered wagon in 1832. They settled in a log house in Westport where Harris farmed, bought land to sub-divide, and served as postmaster.

In 1846 he acquired from A. B. H. McGee an inn (originally John McCoy's store and William Chick's) on the northeast corner of Westport road and Pennsylvania avenue. Much expanded and renamed Harris House, his hotel became the last outpost of civilization on the way west. Renowned for its generous hospitality, bounteous southern cooking and strict ban on dancing (Mrs. Harris did not approve), everybody who was anybody came there. With the Santa Fe Trail running past its front door and the Boone-Bernard Trading Post (today's Kelly's Tavern) west across the street, it was the place to meet in Westport.

Col. Harris had bought a 53-acre farm running from 34th to 39th streets, Main to Gillham road, and in 1855, on a low terrace at its southwest corner, he built a fine eight-room two-story brick home. Facing north at the intersection of Westport road and Main street, it was a classic Greek Revival structure with detached kitchen. Its bricks were of Westport clay and its beams of Westport walnut.

Unfortunately Westport's glory years were few and by 1859 the town had peaked. Times were bad and border incidents were flaring when the Harrises left their fine manse, not to return for ten years. When the Civil War erupted, both Harris' home and hotel were occupied by Union troops. After the war, aging John Harris was no longer host of the Harris House hotel.

The seven Harris girls were married, and the 16 Harris slaves were freed when the Colonel and his wife returned to their home together with daughter Josephine, her husband Charles Kearney and their three children. Urgently needing more space, a two-story, six-room wing with veranda was added to the rear of the original house in 1870.

But time was running out for John Harris who died four years later on August 7, 1874 at age 75. Today his stately home lives on. Once moved (in 1922 in two sections, two blocks distant), twice converted to business use, now on its third try at becoming a house-museum, it stands at 40th street and Baltimore avenue.

67

VASSIE·JAMES·WARD·HILL
MARCH·29·1875
JUNE·23·1954

# Mrs. A. Ross Hill

*1875-1954*

Pem-Day & Sunset Hill

Mrs. A. Ross Hill, a native Kansas Citian, was born Vassie James on March 29, 1875, a sister of T. M. James, whose china company many Kansas Citians remember. Following in her mother's footsteps, Vassie attended Vassar, graduating in 1897. The next year she married Hugh Campbell Ward, son of pioneer Seth Ward, whose graceful 1872 home stands on 55th street just east of Ward Parkway.

Hugh Ward died in 1909, and Vassie James Ward married educator A. Ross Hill, a native of Nova Scotia. He was then president of the University of Missouri (1908-1921), later president of the Kansas City Real Estate Board, and 1933-34 mayoral candidate for the new "Citizens Fusion" party, in which he was soundly trounced by the Pendergast machine.

Mrs. Hill had three sons and a daughter—an average household for the time, except there was *nothing* average about Mrs. A. Ross Hill. Education was her prime interest and deepest concern. She wanted her children to have an education along the lines of the prestigious eastern boarding schools. She believed more attention should be paid to what children did in their leisure time. And she espoused quicker acceptance of new teaching techniques.

Mrs. Hill was not one to want and wonder. In 1910 she had three school-age sons when, with the help of a dozen Kansas City businessmen, she started a private school for boys called Country Day. Its first year classes were held in the then vacant John Wornall house at 61st terrace and Wornall road, with an enrollment of 20. In three years there were 52. What became Pembroke-Country Day School for Boys was off and running.

By 1913 Mrs. Hill's daughter needed an education too. So using her home at 800 West 52nd street as the schoolroom, Sunset Hill, a private school for girls, was born. Mrs. Hill was simply doing what came naturally.

Lest you wonder, Mrs. Hill, contrary to the seemingly obvious, was not named for her alma mater. Rather, she bore the given name of a friend of her mother, known as "Aunt" Vassie, although not actually related. So much for myth.

Vassie James Ward Hill died at age 79 on June 23, 1954, but her vision lives on. Pem-Day and Sunset Hill, the products of her doing, have come full circle. A long-planned merger of the two schools is taking place, and Mrs. A. Ross Hill's private school for boys and separate school for girls will be one.

# Mary Rockwell Hook

*1877-1978*
Architect

I t's a special person, indeed, who makes it to age 101, still under his own power. But to expire *on* one's 101st birthday takes perfect timing as well.

Mary Rockwell Hook was special, and her timing was perfect. Born September 8, 1877 in Junction City, Kansas, she was one of five lively, talented and independent daughters of former Union Army Captain and Mrs. Bertrand Rockwell. A successful merchant, grain mogul and bank executive, Rockwell moved his family to Kansas City in 1906.

Mary Rockwell was then 29, a Wellesley graduate, seasoned traveler, and architect. When she decided architecture was her forte, with the support and encouragement of her family, she enrolled in the Chicago Art Institute's department of architecture. Not surprisingly, she was the only female entrant. Study in Boston followed, and in Paris at Ecole des Beaux Arts.

In Kansas City the family's first priority was for a large home. Mary, ripe for practical experience, got her first big job on their three-acre homesite in the rolling Sunset Hill district. There she built her family's large rectangular two-story stucco house inlaid with timbers. That neighborhood became the cradle for her work.

In 1907 after being turned down by Wight & Wight, Mary Rockwell signed on with the architectural firm of Howe, Hoit and Cutler. The following year she formed her own firm with partner Mac Remington. Their distinctive stone and brick mansions bristle locally from Sunset Hill's rocky terrain to rural Raytown. In Florida she developed 55 acres of beachfront on Siesta Key in Sarasota; in Harlan County, Kentucky she created Pine Mountain settlement school.

Kansas City's Rockwell Lane, a short curvy hilly street running west and north from Loose Park memorializes her family name. Nearby lies her landmark complex of three homes which sprawl off a circle at 50th and Summit streets. There clustered on a flat hilltop overlooking Brush Creek Mary Rockwell built "Pink House" for re-sale, an Italianate stone for her family, and her own eclectic brick-and-everything crazy-quilt.

Mary Rockwell married Inghram Hook in 1921. He died in 1973; she lived another five years, almost totally blind but still vital, until her 101st birthday. On September 8, 1978, she died at Siesta Key.

71

# Rev. Thomas Johnson

*1802-1865*

## Shawnee Indian Missionary

The Rev. Thomas Johnson, the Methodist minister for whom Johnson County, Kansas is named was full of "firsts". He first came here in 1829, the area's first white settler on the Kansas side. He built the first log house near Turner, establishing the first Indian Mission School there as well. His son, Alexander, was born in 1832, one of the first American citizens born in the territory which became the state of Kansas.

Thomas Johnson was born in Nelson County, Virginia July 11, 1802. He came to this western buffer zone at 27 to teach and preach the Methodist gospel to the Indians. Ten years later in 1839 he had established the largest and most influential outpost in the area—the Shawnee Methodist Mission and Manual Labor School. On 2240 acres of government-granted land (at 53rd street and Mission road in today's Fairway), he and his brother William built a short-lived but potent force on the frontier.

His school accommodated upwards of 100 boarding students in the five main buildings which formed the nucleus of the complex. Out-buildings included a steam flour-and-saw-mill where the Indians brought grain to be ground, and obtained lumber for houses.

In 1854 the first "Bogus" Kansas legislature convened at the mission and Johnson was a delegate. From this point, factionalism tore at the territory. And as hostilities heated-up, the mission declined.

Four years later the Rev. Johnson moved his family from the mission to a farm in Kansas City. His once-proud mission was soon occupied by Union soldiers—a bitter blow to Virginia-born, slave-owning Thomas Johnson. At his new farm living in a large old-style colonial mansion on 600 acres "he opposed secession on the one hand, and coercion on the other." With such fence-sitting sentiments, Johnson was harrassed first by one side and then the other.

Near midnight of New Year's Day 1865 guerillas came to Johnson's farmhouse "asking for directions." A shot was fired through the heavy front door, mortally wounding the minister. Sixty-two year old Thomas Johnson died shortly after. He was quietly buried in the mission cemetery (on today's Johnson drive just west of the Fairway shops) beneath a marker which reads "He built his own monument, which shall stand in peerless beauty long after this marble has crumbled into dust, a monument of good works."

Now three remaining buildings of Johnson's historic Shawnee Mission School are under restoration as a state museum.

73

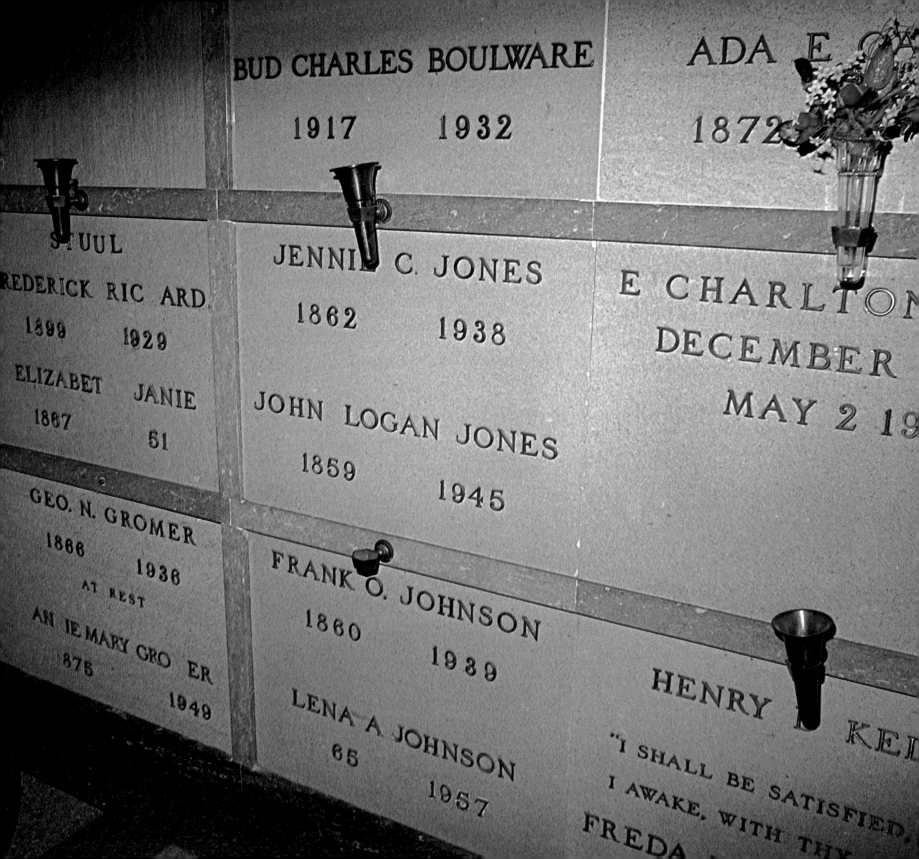

# J. Logan Jones

*1859-1945*

## The Jones Store

"**B**orn in a wigwam and died in a mansion" read one thumbnail biography of John Logan Jones, progenitor of today's Jones Store Company and Kansas City's indomitable merchant prince at the turn of the century.

Jones was born in a wigwam when in 1859 his young parents were in a wagon train en route from Franklin County, Illinois to Lawrence, Kansas. In Ottawa Indian territory, on the banks of the Marais de Cygnes, his expectant mother was taken to the wigwam of an Ottawa Indian Chief named, coincidentally, Jones. There the infant dry goods tycoon first saw light of day.

His parents soon pressed on to Lawrence where they farmed for two losing years before heading back to Illinois. There J. Logan grew up, was educated, taught school and at age 20 set forth from, on his first retailing venture. One by one his Jones stores progressed across Illinois to Kansas, and ultimately to Kansas City.

By 1895 J. Logan Jones had parlayed his humble beginnings into the gigantic seven-story Jones & Company store at the corner of 12th and Main streets. The largest department store in town, it sold groceries, oil, coal, bedding, hardware and clothing, featuring the latest services: a cafe, art gallery, customer banking, and an employee roof garden.

From his baronial mansion "Thornycroft" at 301 East Armour boulevard, the ascetic Jones walked downtown each morning until the financial depression of 1910. It was then, after 15 star-studded years, that his retail fiefdom collapsed into bankruptcy. Jones lost everything—his grand store, its warehouse, thriving mail order business, and his imposing home. In 1912, the Jones & Company store was assumed by New York interests.

The philosophical merchant lost his store but not his spirit. Within three years he had regrouped. And in 1915 at age 56, the feisty little fighter was back in the "rag" business, this time selling close-outs at a newly opened bargain center he called Logan Jones Dry Goods Store (to distinguish it from his "lost Lenore.") Located near 7th and Main streets in the city's "graveyard" area north of the 8th street viaduct, Jones' new store undersold its competition amid a blitz of newspaper advertising studded with J. Logan's little homilies and words of wisdom.

Jones made a financial come-back, retiring 20 years later to Long Beach, California. While on a visit here, he died October 21, 1945 at age 86.

75

# Isaac "Ike" Katz

*1879-1956*

## Katz Drug Stores

"Ike" Katz and his younger brother, partner and best friend, Mike, were an unbeatable pair for more than 50 years. Big brother Ike was a flamboyantly extroverted non-stop talker; Mike was reflective, analytical and restrained. Together they built a memorable midwest cut-rate drugstore kingdom.

Ike Katz' story bears a Tiny Tim flavor. He was born March 8, 1879. As a child he emigrated with his family from Poland. He was poor, little, and crippled. He navigated lifelong with a painful limp, the result of a childhood baseball game gone bad.

His business career began early as a "news butcher", hawking papers and whatever else he could on the Great Northern railroad west and up to the Klondike gold rush in the Yukon. Riding the rails brought him to Kansas City in the 1900s where he and brother Mike set up a fruit stand across from the old Union Depot in the West Bottoms.

From there it was uptown, where the Katz boys opened confectionaries at 12th and McGee streets and at 8th and Grand avenue. During World War I these wondrously metamorphosed into cut-rate "drug stores", underselling everyone else, staying open evenings and Sundays, and purveying everything from patent medicines to (eventually) monkeys. Katz's fame fed on rock-bottom prices, breadth of merchandise, and promotional advertising. Who can forget "Scat to Katz!"? Or the World War I tagline "Katz pays the tax."? Or their black cat's-head trademark?

Ike Katz was slogan-happy. Catchy phrases and curbstone philosophy rolled off his silver tongue. An idea-mad promoter, he organized annual Katz Free Concerts in the 1940s, "buying" the Philharmonic for a day and importing Benny Goodman to perform with it. His zany promotions landed him in TIME magazine when he cut the price of pet monkeys to a close-out $79 in April 1951.

Ike Katz had been in business with Mike 47 years then, and it was just goal to go before they sold their stores to Skaggs. He'd made a bundle and gleefully given much of it away to favorite philanthropies (the Philharmonic, Kansas City Art Institute, Conservatory of Music, and Jewish organizations.)

"A winner never quits, and a quitter never wins" was his pet maxim. In his 77 years Ike Katz *never* quit. In spite (or because) of being poor, little, crippled and a Polish immigrant, he was a winner till the day he died—November 9, 1956.

# Col. Charles E. Kearney

*1820-1898*

Outfitter

Charles Esmond Kearney was born in Ireland March 8, 1820 the son of an Army officer. After "a good education" there, at 17 he set sail for the United States. Here he made directly for Texas where his brother had located, and where for 15 years he engaged in lucrative trade with Mexico before settling here in 1852.

An early boarder at the Harris House hotel in Westport, 32-year old Charles Kearney met and married Josephine Harris, one of the seven lively daughters of hotelkeeper Colonel John Harris. He became a partner in Kearney and Bernard, the major Westport outfitters of wagon trains bound for Oregon and Santa Fe, and opened a wholesale and retail grocery business on the levee downtown.

Kearney saw that the lack of rail connections was holding back our town's development. Together with the entrepreneur Kersey Coates and newpaperman Robert T. Van Horn, Kearney put his savvy to work and in 1866 secured an extension of the Cameron Railroad, a branch of the Hannibal and St. Joseph. When the line was reorganized, Charles Kearney became its first president.

Kansas City then had a railroad, but still no vital river crossing. So the three persuaders descended on Washington. After negotiating, jawboning and arm-twisting they prevailed again, and the Hannibal Bridge, Kansas City's missing link was assured. Its completion in 1869 was a mile-stone for Kansas City as well as for Coates, Van Horn and Kearney.

Kearney spent the later years of his life trying to save intact the Westport farm of his late father-in-law, Col. John Harris. The stately two-story farmhouse stood in the intersection of 40th and Main streets, on the west edge of his farm, and the thoroughfare made a jog around it. Straightening Main became the hue and cry of property owners farther south. The city favored, and Kearney fought what would mean a division of the old Harris farm from its antebellum house.

In the end, Kearney lost his long battle and sold the property which was then resold for development (site of today's Skaggs drug store.) The red brick Harris house of 1855 was moved in two sections, two blocks west where it now stands. Facing east instead of north at 40th street and Baltimore avenue, it is under restoration as an historic house-museum.

The defeated Col. Kearney died January 3, 1898 at age 77.

# William T. Kemper Sr.

*1865-1938*

## Commerce Trust

William Thornton Kemper, Sr., whose family fortune became one of Kansas City's largest, began his career at age 14 on the business end of a broom, sweeping floors in a shoe store in which his father was a partner. Kemper was born in Gallatin, Missouri, November 2, 1865.

Matriculating from shoe store janitor to shoe salesman, young Kemper, representing the St. Joseph concern of Noyes, Norman & Kemper, called on the Valley Falls, Kansas firm of his future father-in-law, Rufus Henry Crosby. There he sold not just the account, but the client's daughter as well when he and Charlotte Crosby were married in 1890. They moved to Kansas City three years later.

Here the 26-year old businessman organized the Kemper Mill and Elevator Company, followed by Kemper Investment Company, and then Kemper Mercantile Company, an early day mail order house. At the turn of the century when Kemper was elected to head the Board of Trade, he was its youngest president ever. He was 33.

From there Kemper went into banking, and every decade became a milestone. Within ten years W. T. Kemper was president of the Commerce Trust Company empire. Ten years later he made a killing, selling the Commerce at the boom price of $220 a share, and ten years later buying it back at $86.

Interestingly enough, one source of Kemper's fortune did not derive from banking, but from the defunct Kansas City, Mexico & Orient Railroad—the shattered dream of Kansas Citian Arthur Stilwell. When that aborted line went under, W. T. Kemper was appointed receiver. Stock of dubious value in the never-completed, disconnected route to the west coast of Mexico was awarded him for that service. In fact, something more than a majority of the reorganized Orient's stock was in his hands when, as luck would have it, oil was discovered along the road's tracks in Oklahoma, Texas and the southwest. Undreamed of value suddenly came to the line (which also transported its own cache of new crude). In 1928 Kemper sold out to the Santa Fe. Such is the stuff dreams are made of.

Money-making Kemper's long suit was interspersed with a modicum of political activity: as Democrat National Committeeman, one-time Democrat mayoral candidate (defeated), and police commissioner. But for the most part, Kemper stuck to his last—banking—until his death at age 72 in January 1938.

81

# George Kessler

*1862-1923*

## Parks & Boulevards

George Kessler shaped the physical face of Kansas City as landscape architect and Park Board secretary. He was sculptor of our soil and plastic surgeon of our parkways. He made beauty out of this beast.

Kessler was born in Frankenhausen, Germany on July 16, 1862. His family came to New York when he was two. He was educated there but returned to Germany, studying gardening, botany and engineering. Afterwards he served a two-year apprenticeship in the gardens of the Grand Duke of Saxe-Weimar before returning to New York City. In New York he worked briefly with Central Park designer Frederick Law Olmstead.

During the mid-1880s Kessler came west as Superintendent of Parks for the Kansas City, Fort Scott & Gulf Railroad expressly to create their amusement park in Merriam, Kansas. His next creation was Kansas City's Hyde Park where he converted an ugly shantytown into a beauty spot south of 36th street on Gillham road.

Nearby, wealthy smelter operator August Meyer hired the young designer to landscape the grounds of his Germanic castle "Marburg" at 44th street and Warwick boulevard (today's Kansas City Art Institute). In 1892 Meyer, president of the Park Board, and his friend William Rockhill Nelson, threw their considerable support behind hiring Kessler as secretary of the Park Board.

At the time, Kansas City had virtually no parks, and no park plan in mind. Kessler's first task was to tackle the unsightly West Bluff—a ragged and smelly hillside slum which was a visitor's first view on leaving the train station in the West Bottoms. There Kessler created West Terrace Park, and the beginnings of Kansas City's Park system.

In 1893 Independence avenue was built to boulevard specifications. Two years later, Gladstone was completed. The next year, The Paseo flowed from 9th to 17th street. By 1900 Cliff Drive, North Terrace Park, Penn Valley Park and Benton boulevard were underway.

In 1902 Kessler stepped down from the Park Board to start his own firm, devoting his genius to cemeteries and college campuses including Mt. Washington, Elmwood and Forest Hill; KU, William Jewell and Washburn.

Kessler's grand plan of public parks and interconnecting boulevards here became the yardstick for city planning. On March 19, 1923 at age 60 George Kessler died and was buried in Bellefontaine Cemetery in St. Louis.

# Frank S. "Dad" Land

*1890-1959*

De Molay

Frank Sherman "Dad" Land was a pied piper and an evangelist from childhood. This man whose name became synonymous with the Order of De Molay was born in Kansas City June 21, 1890. Shortly thereafter his family moved to St. Louis, and during their stay there young Land's evangelism first surfaced.

At the tender age of ten, the magnetic youngster became known locally as the "boy preacher of St. Louis", an appellation derived from the overwhelming success of his afternoon Sunday School classes held in the family basement. Upwards of 300 children flocked there voluntarily to be mesmerized by their articulate and compelling classmate. A timid child at school, Frank Land blossomed on a podium before his peers.

When his family returned to Kansas City, Land attended Manual High School and later, the Kansas City Art Institute by day, and worked evenings in his grandmother's restaurant at 31st and Holmes streets. At 19 he bought the restaurant for himself; soon became a leader of the Municipal Art League; sold his popular restaurant; and in time became a social services executive as an outgrowth of his volunteer work with the Scottish Rite.

Frank Land, not yet 30, was not letting grass grow. Organizational blood coursed through his veins. In 1919 he founded the Order of De Molay, a brainchild of his fertile imagination, named for Jacques De Molay, the last Grand Master of the Knights Templar. (De Molay was the crusader betrayed by Philip the Fair and burned at the stake in front of Notre Dame Cathedral in Paris.)

A youth organization, De Molay was designed to benefit fatherless boys, to appeal to youths 14 to 21, and to promulgate leadership and citizenship in an aura of mystique. Sponsored by the Masons, De Molay was the first new twist in Masonry in 200 years. The time was right, and it caught on, *big.*

From modest local beginnings, De Molay's membership by the end of 1920 stood at 3,000. "Dad" Land became De Molay's first full-time director. He ended up staying 40 years. During that time the order touched the lives of three million men and boys, boasting "alums" ranging from FDR and Walt Disney (a Kansas City native and member), to "Lum & Abner" (Chester Lauck and Norris Goff). At his retirement, Land's creation had spawned 2,000 chapters in 12 countries and in all 50 states.

Frank "Dad" Land died at age 69 on November 8, 1959, dear to the hearts of his "boys", young and old.

85

# John Lazia

*1896-1934*

## Crime Figure

In July 1934 when his luck ran out, Johnny Lazia had been Kansas City's star underworld figure for six precarious years. In 1928 he was appointed to succeed Mike Ross as head of the North Side Democratic Club. That occasioned a big clan gathering at the 5th street and Grand avenue clubrooms, with Ross' lieutenants solemnly swearing their allegiance to "Little Italy" and to their new leader Johnny Lazia. From that time, he'd ridden high.

A dapper, darkly handsome, swaggering little man, he was a showy dresser and heavy gambler; night club owner and dog track operator with a criminal record. No question about it, Lazia was boss of the North Side.

If you bought soft drinks in this town, you were a customer of John Lazia; he controlled soft drink concessions. If you carelessly mislaid a relative, you called John Lazia; he controlled the rackets. So complete was his control here that if you called the police, Johnny Lazia might answer the phone.

When Kansas City businesswoman Nell Donnelly was kidnapped in 1931, her attorney (later husband), Senator James A. Reed, called Lazia and warned him to find her *at once*, and he did. When City Manager H. F. McElroy's daughter, Mary, was kidnapped in 1933, Lazia was given "full charge" of the investigation. The police were ordered to keep hands off, and she too was freed. Lazia, reputedly a close personal friend of the City Manager, was once generously characterized by McElroy as "a political leader of civic spirit, speaking for the poor people of his district." He certainly did.

John Lazia also "spoke" for a good deal more. The Union Station massacre of June 17, 1933 was linked with him. And in August of that year he and one of his lieutenants, Charles Gargotta, barely survived the famed Armour boulevard shoot-out (a case of internecine warfare among factions) by surrendering to Sheriff Tom Bash.

Lazia "spoke" for tax evasion too, on which charge in 1930 he was indicted. When he failed to file a federal return on $82,000 for 1929 he was convicted and sentenced to serve one year in jail— but Pendergast interceded in high places.

So it happened that 37 year old Johnny Lazia was out on appeal when, on July 10, 1934, he was chopped down in a riot of sub-machine gun fire. Charles Carollo inherited Lazia's ward and mantle, which eventually passed on to Charles Binaggio, who died in similar fiery fashion 16 years later.

Today, John Lazia, born John Lazzio, lies buried as John *Lazio* in Mt. St. Mary's.

87

# R. A. Long

*1850-1934*

## Lumber Baron

R. A. Long was a turn-of-the-century lumber baron. Rising to the heights in the building boom of the 1890s, he plunged to the depths in 1929. Even so, Long remains Kansas City's pet captain of industry. His rise was from nothing to something splendid.

Born Robert Alexander Long December 17, 1850 in Shelby County, Kentucky, he came first to Kansas City in 1873. At 22 with $700 he opened a short-lived butcher shop on Broadway near the Coates House. The following year found him haying near Columbus, Kansas.

The year after, Long started his lumber career there, opening his first yard with used lumber and borrowed money. Ten years later he formed Long-Bell Lumber Company with his cousin Victor B. Bell. After opening branches throughout Kansas, headquarters moved to Kansas City in 1892. It was up all the way.

Within 15 years Long built his million-dollar skyscraper, the R. A. Long Building at 10th street and Grand avenue, as capitol of his far-flung kingdom. By then he had a hundred yards in the west and southwest, enormous mill properties, timberland, railroad and steamship lines, coal mines, general merchandising establishments, land agencies, and the entire planned city of Longview, Washington.

R. A. Long was a millionaire of fairy tale proportions. In 1911 he built his most lasting memorial, a 72-room $600,000 Beaux Arts-style mansion at 3218 Gladstone boulevard. Today his stately columned showplace is Kansas City's Museum; then it was called "Corinthian Hall." Four large houses (mansions to most eyes) were moved to clear the square block for Long's palace.

Longview Farms which he created in 1915 near Lee's Summit was icing on Long's cake. With 1700 acres and 40 structures, his private village was one of the most elaborate stock farms in the world. Despite his wealth, R. A. Long was a reserved, unpretentious and deeply religious man. The Independence Avenue Christian Church which he built was his spiritual home.

In 1920 Long was worth tens of millions of dollars. After 1929 his business behemoth crashed. Resisting bankruptcy, he opted for reorganization, confident his company would survive to rise again. But he did not live to see it. On March 15, 1934 at 83, he died.

89

# Ella C. and Jacob L. Loose

### 1860-1945        1850-1923

## Loose-Wiles Biscuit Company

The rise of Sunshine Biscuit king Jacob Loose began when the young Pennsylvania transplant to Chetopa, Kansas opened his first dry goods store there in the 1870s. Twenty-five years later, he had become baking mogul of Kansas City's enormous Loose-Wiles Biscuit Company. Here in the lap of luxury, Jacob and Ella Loose lived well and gave generously.

The Loose's philanthropy is legendary, but two early gifts stand out. Jacob Loose's name evokes lovely Loose Park, the rolling 80-acre green space just south of the Plaza on Wornall road which Mrs. Loose gave the city in 1923 in her husband's memory. Ella Loose herself was synonymous with her 30-year tradition of Thanksgiving "shoe parties." Until the 1940s, Mrs. Loose gave the children at the Gilliss Orphans' Home an annual party, complete with a brand new pair of shoes for each plus a dollar bill for spending!

The Loose name also conjures up lavish living—their 1909 mansion with its hand-wrought bronze Tiffany doors, still standing on the southeast corner of Walnut and Armour boulevard; "Searocks", their seven-acre summer place perched on a low rocky cliff at Gloucester, Massachusetts; Mrs. Loose's apartment in The Walnuts (an entire floor overlooking Loose Park); her winter apartment at the Mayflower hotel in Washington, D. C. from which she launched her career in 1929 as social lioness; and her ultimate 14-room, 7-bath

digs at the Shoreham where she suddenly moved ten years later.

During Jacob Loose's lifetime, the couple's social life was modest, so not surprisingly, after his death, Ella Loose became a social butterfly. At past 60, she went to Washington "to scale the battlements of capital society."

For almost ten winters Ella Loose held sway there from a spacious apartment at the Mayflower hotel until an unpardonable gaffe in the late 1930s. At one of her dinner parties, a brand of tea biscuit made by a cracker company other than her own was served. Mrs. Loose promptly terminated her lease, taking her custom to the Shoreham where she prevailed for another seven years.

Jacob Loose died at "Searocks" at age 73 on September 18, 1923. Ella Loose outlived him almost a quarter of a century, expiring on September 26, 1945 at age 85 in her apartment at The Walnuts. Their combined charitable trusts, together with those of his brother Joseph and family, ultimately formed the basis for today's Kansas City Association of Trusts and Foundations.

# Dr. Johnston Lykins

*1800-1876*

## First Mayor

Dr. Johnston Lykins was a Virginian by birth, a missionary by persuasion, a doctor by profession, and Kansas City's first mayor by default. Dr. Lykins was born August 15, 1800, and came west in 1828 with his bride, Delilah McCoy Lykins; his father-in-law, the Baptist missionary Isaac McCoy; and McCoy's surveyor son, John Calvin—all shepherding their Shawnee Indian parishioners on the long trek from Michigan to Kansas. Dr. Lykins doctored their bodies as well as their souls. He vaccinated his flock against smallpox. And he compiled a Shawnee-English dictionary and written alphabet to enable the Shawnees to read his translation of the Bible as well.

Dr. Lykins was a bit of everything, becoming a key figure in the group of men who launched and guided Kansas City's development. William S. Gregory won the town's first election, but ten months later it was discovered he had not lived the required time in Kansas City and was ineligible. Dr. Lykins, Council President, filled out Gregory's term, and was then elected in his own right the following year.

The city-builder/missionary/doctor/mayor also became one of the incorporators of the Chamber of Commerce and of the Kansas Valley Railroad Company, which he served as president in 1857. He became one of the town's first "capitalists" too as evidenced by the palatial home he built downtown. This once-elegant red brick cube stands much-altered today as the Roslin hotel on the southwest corner of 12th and Washington streets. When completed in 1857 it stood on the southeast corner of 12th and Broadway with two stories, 14 rooms each with 15 foot ceilings, fireplaces and crystal chandeliers galore. Dr. Lykins spent $20,000 on his showplace which soon became a social and political focus of town. It was sold in 1889, moved and a third story added.

Dr. Lykins, a loyal Unionist, died August 15, 1876 at age 76. His second wife, Martha Livingston Lykins, a fanatical secessionist, converted the house into a boarding school for girls. She soon married Lykins' closest friend, George Caleb Bingham who was Missouri's most famous genre and portrait artist. She, together with both husbands, lies in Union Cemetery; Dr. Lykins on one side and Bingham on the other.

# John Calvin McCoy

*1811-1889*

### Founder of Westport

John Calvin McCoy was a "founder" twice over. First of Westport where he settled in 1830, and again eight years later, of the original Town Company of Kansas, which became Kansas City. Looking back in 1880 McCoy candidly stated, "We never dreamed we were founding a city." Whether or not, he and his compatriots threw themselves into this wild place with vigor and dedication. And McCoy, a man of many hats, wore them all for almost 70 years.

Born in Indiana September 28, 1811, schooled in Kentucky as a surveyor at Transylvania University, 19 year old John Calvin McCoy came west in 1830 with his father, the Baptist minister Isaac McCoy. The Reverend McCoy, a missionary to the Indians west of the Missouri river, was accompanied by his daughter, Delilah and her husband, Dr. Johnston Lykins. All settled and invested in what McCoy called Westport, "a portal to the west."

There McCoy wore all his hats: town father, surveyor, tradesman, real estate investor, and subdivider. In February 1835 he patented a tract of government land, surveyed it and filed a plat for his new town of Westport. His first 16½ acres he divided into building lots. But sales were not brisk, so the enterprising McCoy offered freebies. To get settlers he would give a lot to anyone willing to build and live there. It worked, and Westport prospered.

To tap the westward migration, McCoy opened a trading post on the northeast corner of Westport road and Pennsylvania avenue. Leading to it, he hacked a road through the wilderness from Chouteau's landing on the river to his store four miles south.

When the Town Company of Kansas was organized in 1838, John McCoy was there. As one of the 14 original investors, he bought ¹⁄₁₄th of the future downtown district of Kansas City, surveyed the area, and following the second sale, platted the remainder of what had originally been Gabriel Prudhomme's farm. McCoy invested heavily in town lots, was elected secretary of the Company, and its first historian as well. For 40 years Kansas City was his life, except for that sad period during the Civil War when this staunch southern supporter was exiled by Order No. 11.

On September 2, 1889 just 26 days shy of his 78th birthday, John Calvin McCoy, father of two cities, died in his home at 711 Olive street. He was buried in Union Cemetery, not far from three other of Kansas City's 14 founders: William Miles Chick, Jacob Ragan, and William Gilliss.

# James Hyatt McGee

*1786-1840*

## Early Settler

One of Kansas City's earliest settlers was James Hyatt McGee, the first white man to own land within the present city limits. In 1828 he bought 320 acres from the government near Chouteau's warehouse, making him the largest landholder among the original patentees. In ten years, his holdings had tripled.

James Hyatt McGee was born in Virginia on New Year's Day, 1786. He came to Missouri from his Shelbyville, Kentucky farm in 1827. With him were his wife, Eleanor Frye McGee, upwards of a dozen children, and the first slaves in western Missouri.

After a year in Liberty, he brought his bulging household here, settling on a tract of land adjoining the south edge of the original townsite. For four years they lived in a log cabin there while McGee operated a grist mill on the river, under government contract to supply flour to the Indians. Soon he added a distillery to the flour mill and began operating a ferry across the Missouri river as well.

McGee, always "a willing victim to a lasting land hunger", bought more land; built a sawmill; operated a brick kiln; owned a corn cracker; and began lending money. He was soon able to build a new home on his farm near 20th street and Baltimore avenue, the first brick dwelling in the city. Simple but adequate, it had two rooms divided by a dog-trot on either side.

James Hyatt McGee, highly regarded citizen and prosperous businessman was a prolific parent too. Of his multitudinous offspring, two played prominent roles in Kansas City. McGee's eldest son, A. B. H., operated a lucrative business outfitting the westward-bound, including John C. Fremont. It was the calm, reasonable A. B. H. McGee who effected the notable reconciliation between Fremont and his new father-in-law, the tryannical Senator Thomas Hart Benton after Fremont married 15-year old Jessie Benton over her father's objections.

The antithesis of this placid older McGee brother was impetuous, headstrong E. Milton McGee. Milton quarreled with his father and ran away from home at age 16. Striking it rich in California in 1849, Milton returned to become Kansas City's first big real estate developer, of "McGee's Addition." In 1870 Milton McGee also became mayor of Kansas City. And after Elmwood Cemetery opened in 1872, it was he who moved the McGee family graves from the family farm to the new cemetery.

James Hyatt McGee died at age 54, May 26, 1840. His hardy wife, lovingly known as "Mother McGee", outlived him by almost half a century. Having borne sixteen McGees, she died at age 89 on November 22, 1880.

ARTHUR MAG
OCT. 11, 1896 – OCT. 23, 1981

# Arthur Mag

*1896-1981*

Lawyer

Arthur Mag was a very big little man. In stature, at 5′4″, he was downright diminutive. In reputation, he was gargantuan. His passion was law; his driving passion, wills and trusts; and his consuming passion, what became of those. "The dead hand simply cannot direct the future", he maintained.

The cocky, dapper, fast-thinking little legal machine was born October 11, 1896 in New Britain, Connecticut, the son of a men's clothing merchant. At Yale he met Louis Rothschild whose family owned the respected Rothschild's clothing stores here. It was through their friendship that Mag came to Kansas City in the mid-1920s.

Three years out of Yale Law school, Mag cast about here for work, and at the eleventh hour, landed a job as law clerk with Kansas City's prestigious Rozzelle Vineyard Thatcher & Boys.

Of the four major partners in the aging firm, two died within a month of each other. Another had just retired. And the fourth was terminally ill. With no one steering the ship, law clerks and secretaries wondered when the firm would fold.

Arthur Mag's query to a pivotal client saved the day. He was encouraged to approach Paul Stinson, an esteemed Kansas City trial lawyer. Mag briefed the older man on the law firm's precarious situation, and proposed that the two firms merge. Ultimately the hugely successful "law factory" of Stinson Mag McEvers & Fizzell emerged.

Arthur Mag was a peripatetic business lawyer who became a working member of dozens of corporations. This circuitously led to the creation of his wildly innovative trust concept, now much copied. His brainchild began with the Carrie J. Loose Trust which Mag wrote in July 1927. His idea was to establish one overall association to which large individual trusts (such as Mrs. Loose's) would belong. Money would then be funneled into large unfilled community needs. A clearing house of sorts; "enlightened control of large bequests", Mag called it.

The revolutionary concept of the Carrie J. Loose Trust was challenged in court but survived to become a basis for the multi-million dollar Kansas City Association of Trusts and Foundations. Originally Carrie Loose's large nest egg was combined with the enormous Jacob L. and Ella C. Loose Trust plus one or two others. Now Kansas City Association of Trusts and Foundations has become big business, dispensing staggering amounts for philanthropy hereabouts.

On October 23, 1981, twelve days after his 85th birthday, Arthur Mag, the self-winding powerhouse, ran down.

# Alexander Majors

## *1814-1900*
## Wagon Trains

In the 1850s Alexander Majors' name stood for the gigantic freighting firm of Russell, Majors and Waddell, for the short-lived Pony Express, and for that vast network called the Overland Stage Company. Alexander Majors, transportation, and Kansas City were inextricably intertwined, beginning August 10, 1848 when his first wagon train left here for Santa Fe.

Majors, "the great bullwhacker", was born October 4, 1814 in Franklin, Kentucky. Thirty-four years later he ran his first train to Santa Fe— 92 days round trip. Before his star set in 1862, Majors employed upwards of 4,000 men for his 3500 Conestogas which plied the west. He hired a pimply 15 year old lad named Billy Cody, who became one of his most famous Pony Express riders. He wintered 400 horses for the Pony Express near Lee's Summit, and pastured 40,000 oxen on the open range west of State Line now known as Corinth.

On the east side of State Line at 81st street, Alexander Majors built his sturdy white two-story frame farmhouse in 1855-6, as well as his Pony Express relay barn across the line in Kansas. The barn is long-gone, but his house still stands. From his property on State Line, wagon trains loaded with goods from the company's giant warehouse on the riverfront headed west. In Westport, Majors also operated a meat-packing plant supplying wagon trains with cured pork, soap and candles. For almost 15 years Alexander Majors

and his far-flung interests touched the lives of almost everyone here, and of everyone headed west from here.

By 1860, the year the Pony Express began, technology was threatening his operation. Telegraphs and railroads became a reality. It was the telegraph which spelled doom for the Pony Express just as the "great iron horse" would kill Majors' freighting and stage coach operations in time.

In 1865 Majors sold what remained of his diminished freighting interests and moved to Colorado. There 30 years later his former young wagonmaster/Pony Express rider, William F. "Buffalo Bill" Cody encountered his old boss. Majors was living in a log shanty, trying to write his memoirs. Cody salvaged the old man and his pride, helping Majors get his book written ("Seventy Years on The Frontier") and published in 1873. For a time Majors toured as part of Cody's Wild West show, and even lived at Scouts' Rest Ranch in North Platte, Nebraska.

Returning to his old stomping grounds in his last years, Alexander Majors died here at 86 on January 13, 1900. With 15 friends standing by, the great bullwhacker was buried at Union Cemetery.

# Rabbi Samuel S. Mayerberg

*1892-1964*

## Rabbi & Gadfly

Rabbi Samuel Spier Mayerberg was a rare bird. He was outspoken. He took a stand—a thing was either right or it was wrong. He kept a high profile in order to get things done. And he practiced what he preached.

Samuel Mayerberg was born May 6, 1892 in North Carolina, the son of a rabbi. At age 36 he came to Kansas City's Temple B'Nai Jehudah where he was rabbi 32 years. During that action-packed time he was also our civic gadfly, especially so during the political reform of the late 1930s.

A slight square man, Mayerberg was peppery and bright-eyed behind thick glasses; scholarly and articulate; a political hard-hitter; a loyal, devout believer. He believed Jews should remain Jews and not get lost in the melting process. He believed Hitler was all bad. He believed Kansas City's Machine was corrupt.

Mayerberg came into the public eye as a member of the 1931 speakers' bureau supporting the city's proposed "Ten Year Plan." It was a time when "the clergy here was cowed, and racketeers and evil were rampant." His fiery speech to a women's group heralded his initial attack on the city administration and its close connection with organized crime. It was he and the Ministerial Alliance which openly publicized the reform issue and soapboxed before an impassive City Council.

Mayerberg agitated for a recall election in 1932 and formed the short-lived Charter League, forerunner of the Citizens Association. But with little support from the press and the city's leadership, the Charter League died a quick death. For his stance, an assassination attempt was made on Mayerberg's life, and not just once.

After Pendergast's downfall through the courts, the Machine fell too. Samuel Mayerberg was johnny on the spot with clean-up forces to put in a new slate of councilmen. Only after their election in 1940 did charter government become a fact of Kansas City life. Even so, Rabbi Mayerberg remained at the ready.

The scrappy rabbi had his victories as well as defeats. He had his champions and his detractors. He got accolades and brickbats as well. Besides his rabbinical and clean-up activities he was an active, vocal member of the Board of Police Commissioners and of the Philharmonic Association.

Samuel S. Mayerberg, the "conscience of Kansas City" died on November 22, 1964 at age 72.

# August Meyer

*1851-1905*

## Parks

Among Kansas City's "greats", August Meyer, father of our parks and boulevard system is at the top of the heap. It was largely he who made our "city beautiful."

August Meyer was born in St. Louis of German decent August 20, 1851, and came to Kansas City 30 years later. He was educated in Europe (in mining and metallurgy), and became the super-rich mining magnate and co-founder of Leadville, Colorado. By age 30, Meyer had achieved more than most in a lifetime.

In 1875 he opened an ore-crushing mill in Alma, Colorado, and went on, as government assayer, to found nearby Fairplay and Leadville. He and his co-investors (including H. A. W. Tabor of Baby Doe fame) made a fortune. Then in 1881 he opened a smelting plant in the Argentine district here which in eight years' time provided employment for 1,000 men.

The wealthy and successful Meyer was an avid outdoorsman and nature enthusiast. To him, city beautification was imperative, "a community must attract with more than just tax concessions and columns of figures."

Small wonder then as early as 1887 he began working on a major Kansas City parks program. A comprehensive plan of civic improvement was what he and a few others began hammering at. He and his crusading newspaper-owning neighbor, William Rockhill Nelson, beat the drum hard, and

in 1892 Mayor Ben Holmes appointed the city's first Park Board. It was composed of blue-ribbon talent: Meyer (who became president), architect Adriance Van Brunt, Louis Hammerslough who was a leading merchant, industrialist S. B. Armour, and real estate giant William C. Glass.

Meyer and his Park Board hired George Kessler, a talented young landscape architect as secretary. It was Kessler who drew the brilliant masterplan that has become the park system we know today. When the Park Board proposed a special property tax to fund the system, there were howls of protest. But thanks to Nelson's Kansas City STAR and the persuasive Park Board members themselves, funding legislation passed in 1895. The rest is history, with our park system becoming a prototype in the United States.

August Meyer, the leading light in making Kansas City beautiful died at age 54 on December 1, 1905. Meyer Boulevard memorializes his name, as does a lovely wrought iron Tiffany rood screen at Grace and Holy Cathedral given by his wife. His "Marburg", a three-story, 35-room Germanic castle and eight and one-half rolling acres, became the Kansas City Art Institute campus at 44th and Warwick boulevard. August Meyer's presence is still very much with us.

# William Rockhill Nelson

*1841-1915*

Kansas City STAR

William Rockhill Nelson's Kansas City STAR-studded rise to power began March 7, 1841 when Nelson was born in Fort Wayne, Indiana to a wealthy farm family. The smart, rich, tempestuous kid grew into a big, brash lawyer who never practiced; a dilettante of failures; a young adult with little focus. Dismissed from Notre Dame, Nelson had worked half-heartedly on his father's farm; failed in construction; unsuccessfully farmed; and, knowing nothing about newspapering, bought the Fort Wayne SENTINEL.

Nelson, the late-bloomer, came here in 1880 at age 39. He founded the four-page daily Kansas City EVENING STAR, and really succeeded for the first time in his life. In three months, his 2¢ paper had the largest circulation in town. Almost from taws, he plumped for city betterment, crusaded for parks and boulevards, and pushed for municipal reform. "Public improvement mad", some said.

His editorial crusade for city beautification began in 1881. Kansas City with a population of 65,000 had no public parks. His newspaper was barely a year old, but Nelson already had strong, well-placed allies. Together with August Meyer (the Park Board's first president), Nelson persuaded the skilled landscape architect, George Kessler, to become the Board's secretary. And Kansas City's remarkable parks and boulevard system was the happy result.

In a lesser-known role, Nelson was a real estate developer. His first venture in 1883 was a row of small houses on the south side of 31st street between Walnut and Grand avenue, now gone. DeGroff Way, north from 31st street between McGee and Oak came next—a street of attractively-sited modest houses, still extant. Farther south are his Pierce and Houston street houses, and those on 47th street and on Harrison, many of which with their native rock walls remain today. Nelson's capstone was his Rockhill District of two- and three-story houses built for wealthy prospects. This fashionable residential neighborhood north of 47th street and east of Rockhill road is now in a renaissance.

To the northwest of this hilly area, between Oak and Rockhill road south of 45th street, William Rockhill Nelson built his own fabled Oak Hall, a baronial manse which sprawled on 20 acres. When the "Baron of Brush Creek" died at age 74 on April 13, 1915, Oak Hall was dismantled in accordance with his wishes. And in 1930 the splendid new Nelson Gallery of Art rose in its place, constructed with funds provided by the estates of his family. Inside was an art collection purchased with Nelson's $12 million estate, now much refined and augmented, a jewel in Kansas City's crown.

107

# George H. Nettleton

*1831-1896*

## Railroads & Nettleton Home

The name George Nettleton is most closely allied today with the Nettleton Home for Women. But during his lifetime, Nettleton's name and railroading were one. He, as much as any other one person, made Kansas City a great railroad center. Now almost no one remembers.

Born in Chicopee Falls, Massachusetts November 13, 1831, George Nettleton came west in 1857, beginning his railroad career at age 26 as resident civil engineer of the Hannibal & St. Joseph Railroad. Fourteen years later he organized the first Kansas City Stockyards Company, putting up the early frame Livestock Exchange building at 16th and Bell streets. By age 45 he was president and general manager of the old Fort Scott & Memphis road, later to become the Frisco.

When 64-year old George Nettleton died 20 years later on March 26, 1896, he left his widow monetarily very comfortable. Five years before, they had built a beautiful 12 room gray brick mansion on Quality Hill. It perched on the high bluffs overlooking Nettleton's rail and stockyard interests in the West Bottoms below. But widowed Julia Nettleton had no desire to live on there alone. Much as she had loved their home, she gave it away.

In 1890 the Women's Christian Temperance Union had founded the Protestant Home for Aged Women on the old Holmes farm at Independence avenue and Lowell street. Organized to provide shelter and care "for aged women and friendless girls", happenstance changed all that. Thirteen days before the facility was to open, a policeman knocked on the Home's as yet unopened doors, with a destitute woman in tow. Could they, would they take in this homeless person? She was neither aged nor a girl, so hardly fit their format. But since she had nowhere to go, the Home fitted its format to her.

A year later the Home moved to larger quarters at 29th and Cherry streets. And nine years after, their third move was to George Nettleton's mansion on Quality Hill. Reincorporated as the George H. Nettleton Home for Aged Women, its 31 ladies moved in the same day Julia Nettleton moved out (to the Woodlea apartment hotel at 3552 Broadway where she lived for 23 years.)

In 1914, banker E. F. Swinney gave land on Swope parkway at 51st street for the present Nettleton Home. Still supported by endowment and admission fees, the Nettleton Home is as viable now as then, a living memorial to a distinguished figure in Kansas City's early railroad life and to his benevolent widow.

# Ernest H. Newcomb

*1886-1979*

## University of Kansas City

Without Ernest H. Newcomb, there would have been no University of Kansas City; not in the fall of 1933. It was Newcomb's know-how, diplomacy and perseverance combined with businessman-philanthropist William Volker's backing and encouragement that created what is now the University of Missouri at Kansas City.

Newcomb was born in Troutsville, Virginia, September 18, 1886. After an early career as superintendent of county schools in rural Missouri, in 1922 he became president of Central College for Women in Lexington, Missouri. Three years later, the church withdrew its financial support and prepared to merge its three Missouri colleges into one, moving Central to Fayette.

To save his college and his presidency, Ernest Newcomb came to Kansas City to test the water, hopeful of starting a new Methodist college here. What he found was an atmosphere ripe for a university. So ripe, in fact, there were soon two separate groups working hard toward the same goal. One was denominational (Newcomb's Methodist proposal); the other, a broad-based non-sectarian plan.

Newcomb, who had worked diligently for a Methodist-backed Lincoln and Lee University, walked a fine line between the two before finally committing himself to the non-sectarian plan in 1929. This "pearl of great value", as he regarded it, became, four years later, the University of Kansas City—with the enormous financial support of William Volker and broad backing from the community.

Volker donated land for a campus at 50th and Holmes streets, and Newcomb donated his time. All told he worked eight years toward his dream; three of them spent writing every word of the KCU charter, recruiting faculty, designing the initial curriculum and outlining courses. In the fall of 1933, the University of Kansas City came into existence in the old Dickey mansion, with 268 students and a faculty of 18.

Newcomb stayed on as business manager of the University and executive secretary to the Board. But four years later, Newcomb was suddenly out. He left in 1938 not to set foot on the campus for almost 40 years. Meanwhile he founded the Kansas City Town Hall Forum, and for what seemed like forever, the dapper scholarly little gentleman presented an endless string of speakers on his downtown lecture series.

In November 1977 when he was 91, Newcomb was publicly acknowledged by the University for the first time, by the Alumni Association. Two years later, on November 12, 1979, Ernest H. Newcomb, father of KCU died, neglected for 40 years.

NICHOLS

JESSE CLYDE NICHOLS
AUGUST 23,     FEBRUARY 16,
1880              1950

# J. C. Nichols

*1880-1950*

## Country Club Plaza

Jesse Clyde Nichols proved that beauty and good taste can be made to pay. His Country Club Plaza, the grand-daddy of surburban shopping centers, was Nichols' high-water mark. It became Kansas City's star attraction.

J. C. Nichols was born August 23, 1880 on a farm near Olathe, Kansas. From his high school years he was "tight wound and always on the go." Working his way through KU, between his junior and senior years he took an un-grand tour, bicycling through Europe. It made a profound impression on him, his life's work, and on Kansas City.

Nichol's first business venture, a grandiose scheme for colonizing vast sub-marginal farm areas in the southwest and Mexico, was a complete bust. Returning to Kansas City, in 1905 he bought his first tract in the south part of town, ten acres near 51st street and Grand avenue, which he turned into our first suburban development. Nichols began small, but at his death 45 years later, he owned attractive real estate developments on both sides of State Line, from his Country Club Plaza south to who-knows-where.

J. C. Nichols was a sensitive and creative man, agitating tirelessly for comprehensive development. And to achieve it, he hired the best talent to produce it—urban designer George Kessler; landscape architects Hare & Hare; architects Edward Buehler Delk and Edward W. Tanner. Zoning was practically Nichols' middle name. He harped on the subject until the city finally passed its first local zoning ordinance in 1923.

Nationally, J. C. Nichols was regarded as an exemplary urban planner, "a dollar-conscious creative genius." From 1926 until 1948 he served on the National Capital Park and Planning Commission which was charged with restoring the city of Washington to the original vision of L'Enfant. Without him and the Commission, even larger chunks of Washington, D. C. would now be gone.

In Kansas City, Nichols' credits include his quietly acquiring the property for the Liberty Memorial, then selling to the city at cost. As one of three trustees of the William Rockhill Nelson bequest, he was a force in the creation of the Nelson-Atkins Museum of Art. When the Kansas City Art Institute was floundering downtown, Nichols assumed its presidency and made it viable. In 1940 he went to Washington, a member of the Advisory Council on National Defense, and returned with four huge defense plants for this area. He was instrumental in the establishment of Midwest Research Institute here.

J. C. Nichols lived 69 years—long enough to see his beautiful tree bear tender fruit before he died February 16, 1950—our genius of suburban development.

113

# Leroy "Satchel" Paige

*c.1904-1982*

## Baseball Pitcher

Leroy Robert Paige became "Satchel" as a kid in Mobile. The seventh of 11 children, he began work carrying suitcases at the Union Station after school. Figuring if he carried more bags faster, he'd get better tips, young Paige devised a sling harness contraption for hustling several bags at once. The other redcaps hooted and said he looked like a "walking satchel tree." Thus Leroy became Satchel. And Satchel became a legend.

Paige was born July 7, 1904, or was it 1906? He was never quite sure because "My birth certificate was in our Bible . . . and the goat ate the Bible . . . That goat lived to be 27." Fortunately, Paige lived to be 73 (or was it 75?)

His baseball career spanned 40 years ("I've played more baseball than any man alive."), and Kansas City was his home off and on for longer than that. In the late 1930s when first baseman Paige hurt his arm barnstorming in Mexico it looked like the end of the line. Then came a call from the Kansas City Monarchs to pitch. He came here and began a 27 year second career in baseball. Farewell to first base; hello pitching—at age 33 (or so.)

In Paige's long baseball life were three Big Moments—when he pitched a 5-0 shut-out for Cleveland against Chicago in 1948; when he was inducted into baseball's Hall of Fame in 1971; and when he attended the dedication of Satchel Paige Stadium here just three days before he died.

Interspersed was all life's infill which Paige viewed philosophically. Of his reform school stay at age 12 he mused, "It got me away from the bums. It gave me a chance to polish up my baseball game. It gave me some schooling I'd of never taken if I wasn't made to go to class."

Paige had a penchant for sleek cars (and speeding tickets); spiffy clothes (at 6'4½" he wore them with authority); practical jokes; outdoor life; and his wife, LaHoma and their brood of eight.

Theatrics were a part of him. In 1958 he rode a horse in a movie, "The Wonderful Country." In 1968 Paige was sworn in as Deputy Sheriff in the civil division; the week prior, Paige filed for the Democrat nomination in Jackson County's 11th legislative district to run against Leon Brownfield. Satchel Paige was game for anything new. As he always said, "Don't look back. Something may be gaining on you." So Paige looked forward, and had a fine time.

Leroy Robert Satchel Paige, baseball's fastball king, died June 8, 1982. Appropriately his final ride was in a "sleek car", a beautiful 1938 black Packard hearse, en route to Forest Hill Cemetery and burial on Paige Island there.

CHARLES PARKER, JR.
AUGUST 29, 1920
MARCH 12, 1955

# Charlie "Yardbird" Parker

*1920-1955*

## Jazz Great

Since chickens are yardbirds, and Charlie Parker was a fried chicken freak, "Yardbird" Parker evolved—or so one version of his legend goes. Another is since he played like a bird and/or lived free as one, he was known as "Bird" Parker. Take your pick.

Whichever, Parker's life was a classic case of too much and too fast. He lived his almost 35 years in perpetual motion. Born Charles Parker, Jr. in Kansas City, Kansas August 29, 1920, he died like any other junkie in New York on March 12, 1955. One writer summarized, "His is the story of an absent father, a mother who spoiled him, poverty, great sensitivity, and the resulting personality that demanded and fed on excesses until they destroyed him."

At age seven Parker came to Kansas City and began studying music. Academics were not his bag (he "spent three years in high school and ended up a freshman"), but he did play baritone horn in high school band. By age 15 he was serious about the alto sax, playing regularly at Kansas City's Green Leaf Gardens.

A year later, in 1936, Parker married—at age 16. In 1937 he was playing with Jay McShann here; the same year he became a father. Two years later he met Dizzy Gillespie, and the year following, at age 20, said good-bye to Kansas City.

In the big time in the Big Apple he went from marriage to marriage, from booze to drugs, while playing with the greats—Earl "Fatha" Hines, Cootie Williams, Billy Eckstine, and Dizzy Gillespie. Parker's fluid style on alto sax and his inspired solo work brought him international acclaim. "The greatest alto saxophonist in the world" was also versatile, playing tenor sax, doubling on clarinet, and experimenting on practically every brass and woodwind known to man. He had talent—he fathered "be-bop"; and style—his "Cherokee" is a classic; but no discipline.

A mental hospital stay of seven months came between a stint with Dizzy Gillespie in 1944 and playing with Norman Granz' "Jazz at the Philharmonic." He bounced back, and two years later was leading his own group on the west coast. In New York City, Birdland opened in 1949, immortalizing his name and his inimitable style. But a suicide attempt landed him in New York's Bellevue Hospital in 1954. Amazingly, the following year he played again at Birdland, his last engagement. The next week he was dead.

Charlie Parker expired, completely burnt-out at 34½. His funeral was held in Adam Clayton Powell's Abyssinian Baptist church in Harlem. He was brought back to Kansas City for burial, his friends Dizzy Gillespie and Norman Granz helping pay his way.

117

# Chief Joseph Parks

*1794-1859*

## Indian Chief

When Joseph Parks first set eyes on Kansas 152 years ago, all of northeast Johnson County and then some was a Shawnee Indian Reservation totalling 1,600,000 acres; a strip roughly 25 miles north and south and 120 miles east and west.

In the Treaty of 1854 the Shawnees re-ceded to the government all but 200,000 acres. Those they kept for their homes; roughly 200 acres per member. Out of this settlement Joseph Parks, head chief of the Shawnees, and his family got 1280 acres straddling present-day Johnson and Wyandotte Counties west from the state line.

Joseph Parks was an interesting paradox who, depending on his whim, was a full-blood Shawnee, part Indian, or a white man who had been captured by the Indians when very young! Whatever the truth, he enjoyed the advantages and respect of both Indian and white camps.

Parks was born in 1794 probably in Michigan (Shawnee territory) and raised with the family of Gen. Lewis Cass. Educated in Cass' home, Parks served as the General's interpreter until 1831 when he was appointed interpreter for the Shawnee Chiefs' delegation to Washington. Two years later he helped move his people from Ohio to the newly opened Shawnee reservation here. Subsequently he spent several years in Washington as an agent of his tribe, trying to recover money owed them from their various forced hegiras.

Returning to Kansas, Parks settled here on the southeast corner of what became his well-improved farm. In 1845 he built a substantial two-story brick house that stood, until 1905, on the crest of the hill where Pem-Day's tennis courts are today.

He became actively involved in the Rev. Thomas Johnson's Shawnee Methodist Mission and Manual Labor School, joining that faith and the Masons Westport Lodge. Interestingly, Parks was the only slave-owner in Kansas Territory besides the Rev. Johnson.

On May 10, 1854 Parks returned to Washington as a signer of the Treaty giving back to the United States most of the Shawnee reservation here. This newly repossessed land was put up for sale by the government and quickly devoured by pioneers flocking west. The following year, Johnson County was organized.

Chief Joseph Parks died at age 65 on April 4, 1859. He was buried in that all-but-forgotten graveyard on dead-end 59th terrace east of Nieman road.

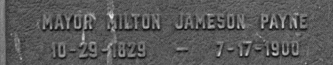

MAYOR MILTON JAMESON PAYNE
10-29-1829    —    7-17-1900

MAYOR OF KANSAS CITY—1855 TO 1859 AND
1862. ONE OF OUR OUTSTANDING PIONEERS
OF THIS GREAT CITY. HE WAS RESPONSIBLE
FOR THE FIRST GRADING OF STREETS
BEYOND THE LEVEE AND FOR OBTAINING
THE FIRST GAS AND WATER PLANTS.
HE ALSO SERVED IN THE MISSOURI
LEGISLATURE WHERE HE HAD CHARGE OF
THE BILL THAT BROUGHT THE FIRST
RAILROAD TO KANSAS CITY.

THIS PLAQUE TO HONOR HIM PLACED BY
THE NATIVE SONS OF KANSAS CITY MISSOURI

# Col. Milton J. Payne

*1829-1900*

## Early Mayor

Col. Milton Jamison Payne, Kansas City's bewhiskered third mayor, served six terms. He completed the 1855 term of John Johnson and was elected five times more. Small wonder he was known as the "father of public improvements." In 1855, since nothing was "improved" here, he had nowhere to go but up.

In 1850, our city's forerunner which was called the Town Company of Kansas, had been organized out of Gabriel Prudhomme's riverfront farm. Three years later, a faulty charter led to reincorporation and a name change, and the City of Kansas was born. Milton Payne was elected to its first City Council when the town's assessed valuation was $54,000; its treasury contained $7.22.

A Kentuckian by birth on October 10, 1829, Payne was out on his own at 13. Apprenticed in printing, he later worked as a dry goods salesman. In 1850 he came here and worked with William Chick in his dry goods store. In time Payne married Mary Adeline Prudhomme, youngest daughter of the late Gabriel Prudhomme from whose farm our city evolved.

In 1854 Payne went to St. Louis to buy a printing press, returned and established the KANSAS CITY ENTERPRISE, which Robert Van Horn later bought, renaming it KANSAS CITY JOURNAL OF COMMERCE. In 1856, a year after Milton Payne became mayor, he retired from business to devote himself to the city.

Payne was a city expansion and betterment buff. During his administrations the first bond issue of $10,000 for public improvements passed, and in 1858 another for $100,000 was voted. The latter was earmarked to grade the bluff and widen and pave the levee, grade and macadamize streets, and build the first city hall.

Payne was the city's first political organizer too, from mayor to state legislator. Politics, railroads, real estate, utilities, transport systems, newspapers, Milton Payne was involved in them all. Too much so for his modest finances, for in 1889, a year before his death, he filed bankruptcy. Payne spread himself too thin, but not his devotion to Kansas City.

On July 17, 1900 he died at age 70. Forty-three years earlier, as an organizing member of the original Union Cemetery Company, Milton Payne had been elected its first president. Fittingly, he lies buried there.

121

# Tom Pendergast

*1872-1945*

## Machine Boss

Thomas J. Pendergast rose to power here on the shoulders of his older brother Jim. Sixteen years older, Jim had come here from their native St. Joseph and in 1882 opened a saloon in the West Bottoms near the old Union Station.

There Jim fed, soothed, helped and guided a loyal clientele, becoming the policemans' friend along the way. "If you feed a man, he'll always be your friend—and vote your ticket." From saloon-keeper to ward boss to Democrat city councilman was the big Irish Catholic's progression. It was to be likewise for younger brother Tom, but in spades.

Tom at age 18 came here as his brother's bookkeeper-cashier, and soon-to-be deputy constable in Jim's First Ward. In time Tom got into real estate leasing downtown, operated the Hasty & Hurry Messenger Service, and finally his own saloon on 12th street.

In 1910 following brother Jim's retirement from public office, Tom was elected to the City Council. He served five years, oiling his machine, retiring in 1915 to devote himself exclusively to his Jackson County Democratic Club. As the Club's president from 1925 until 1938, the City Council was under Tom's complete control. From his dumpy little second-story office at 1908 Main street, he came to control state government too, from governor on down.

Pendergast's reign spanned three decades. Graft, crime and rackets; speak-easies, prostitution and gambling; ghost votes, rigged elections and kick-backs were our lot. We had Tom's ubiquitous Ready-Mix Concrete Company and the paving of Brush Creek; the T. J. Pendergast Wholesale Liquor Company; his notorious old Jefferson hotel operated for fun and profit; and Riverside Race-track which Tom owned, together with a string of racing horses.

Horse-racing and betting on the bang-tails was a passion with Tom Pendergast second only to power. When the jig was up for him, the Fed's figures revealed that in 1935 he had actually wagered $2 million on the horses, losing $600,000.

But Tom Pendergast's ultimate fall was triggered by a 1929 indiscretion. A Missouri fire insurance scandal and reported kick-back ($315,000 to Pendergast personally) lead in 1935 to a tax investigation. On Good Friday, April 7, 1939, the Federal Grand Jury indicted Pendergast. He later pleaded guilty and was sentenced to 15 months in prison, fined $10,000 and payment of $430,000 in back taxes. Within a year he was free.

Tom Pendergast died January 26, 1945 at 72, just a few weeks before his five-year probation was up.

# Elmer F. Pierson

*1896-1982*

## Vendo Company

It was appropriate that in 1966 Elmer Frank Pierson was one of 12 winners of the Horatio Alger awards. While his rise was hardly a saga of rags-to-riches, it was, indeed, remarkable. From grocery clerk in his father's store at 28th and Jarboe streets to vending machine mogul, Pierson and his Vendo Company touched as many lives as some monarchs.

Pierson, a second generation Swede, was born in Kansas City on August 27, 1896. His father, who had sung with the Royal Opera in Stockholm, landed in New York at age 21, came to Kansas City, and opened a grocery on the West Side. Eventually he parlayed it into a three-store chain.

Elmer Pierson attended Kansas City School of Law, but instead of practicing, contacts made in his father's grocery led him into a career as traveling wholesale grocery salesman. Soon tiring of that, Pierson went into real estate (his first fling was a bust), mortgage banking, and insurance.

But vending machines were his trump card. In the 1930s the idea of a machine that would dispense bottled drinks cropped up in the little model and tool shop of J. E. Hagstrom at 17th and Walnut streets. By 1937 it was an idea in search of a manufacturer. The Piersons, Elmer and brother John, latched onto it, founding The Vendo Company which after World War II was the largest manufacturer of vending machines in the world. Right here in River City! The Piersons

retired 37 years later, their "tin boxes" dispensing everything from the Coca-Cola bottles they were invented to serve, to you-name-it.

Bright ideas made Elmer Pierson rich, and Elmer Pierson made Kansas City a co-recipient. As a member of the Board of Governors of the Kansas City Art Institute, he aided and abetted in adding a school of design to its curriculum. A Philharmonic fund-raiser, he diplomatically twisted arms belonging to big donors. As president of the Chamber of Commerce, he was the ambassador of culture's worth to the city. He gave the Nelson-Atkins Museum of Art its sculpture garden after having admired its prototype in Europe. At the former University of Kansas City he provided $250,000 for a student center/lecture hall/meeting place. He established the John B. Gage Lecture and Fellowship Fund honoring our "clean-up" mayor.

In his 85 years Elmer B. Pierson, grocery salesman, lawyer, realtor, mortgage banker, insurance man, manufacturer, made lots of money. The nice thing is, he did such laudable things with it before he died on February 15, 1982.

We know neither when nor where Gabriel Prudhomme was born. Nor when he died, nor where. Alas even his grave is lost to history. In truth, we know precious little about this key figure in Kansas City's birth. Yet we owe it all to him.

Gabriel Prudhomme was French, probably from St. Louis, perhaps one of the tradesmen and followers of Francois Chouteau who came here in the spring 1821. Prudhomme settled with his wife and six children on a farm on the river which "included a natural rock landing on the south bank, immediately below the mouth of the Kaw." In 1831 he paid $340 for 257 acres. There, not far from Chouteau's fur station, Prudhomme farmed and operated a ferry from his rock ledge, but only for ten months. In November 1831, Gabriel Prudhomme was killed, supposedly in a barroom brawl.

The boundaries of Prudhomme's farm ran from the river south to Independence avenue; from Broadway to Troost. The old ASB Bridge approaches (presently being dismantled) approximately divide it down the middle. A key piece of land, it "lay mostly on level ground along the river, its southern edge sloping up 120 feet." Most importantly, it contained that natural rock ledge, ideal for a boat landing.

This then was the original townsite which 14 investors bought in 1838, seven years after Prudhomme's death. The first sale of his farm on July 7 was set aside due to irregularities. A second was held on November 14 with the members of the Town Company of Kansas bidding $4220 for the acreage: William L. Sublette, Moses G. Wilson, John C. McCoy, William Gilliss, Fry P. McGee, Abraham Fonda, William M. Chick, Oliver Caldwell, George W. Tate, Jacob Ragan, William Collins, James Smart, Samuel C. Owens, and Russell Hicks.

The Town of Kansas was finally incorporated in 1850 with a population of 700. Growth was so

# Gabriel Prudhomme

*17??-1831*

## Kansas City's Townsite

slow that for five years the entire metropolis still lay within the farm's boundaries. Under a new charter of February 22, 1853, the town's name became the City of Kansas. The west half of Prudhomme's property remained the city's "downtown" section, and the east half—stretching toward Independence —was residential dotted with neighborhood businesses. By 1857 levee lots which had sold for $200 to $300 in 1838 were fetching $10,000. The city had caught on.

Within the original boundaries of Prudhomme's farm would be built our first two city halls; the still-extant Board of Trade building, the Ebenezer, and Pacific House hotel. Here also would come the early city markets, Gilliss House hotel and Gilliss Opera House. Much later, Tom Pendergast's infamous Jefferson hotel, Annie Chambers' house of ill-repute, the Marble Hall gambling den, William Volker's giant company warehouse and the Rich-Con hardware buildings;

and in recent times, dear Mr. Aron's bag company and the River Quay revitalization effort.

Gabriel Prudhomme died in "a brutal and sudden manner", leaving his farm, a ferryboat (later sold for $85), six children and a pregnant wife. Adeline, who was born the year following her father's death, grew up to marry Milton J. Payne, Kansas City's third mayor (1855-1862) and the "father of city improvements."

Gabriel Prudhomme was buried in the first Catholic Cemetery near 11th street and Broadway. When that cemetery was closed in 1880, his grave was moved or simply lost. Nine years later, in 1889 our city's name was changed for the third and final time to Kansas City. Gabriel Prudhomme's farm remained its heart.

# Dr. Katharine Richardson

*c.1860-1933*

Children's Mercy Hospital

Mercy Hospital's founder and complete dictator for 20 years was a lady medical doctor named Katharine Berry Richardson. On June 1, 1897 she and her sister, Dr. Alice Berry Graham, a dentist, started what became Children's Mercy when they found a crippled waif on the street, carried it home and saw to its care.

This remarkable pair came from Flat Rock, Kentucky. Katharine was born September 28, but never divulged the exact year, thought to be 1860. "Don't ever tell anyone your age; they'll want to retire you", she said. In May 1933 when she was in her seventies, she performed plastic surgery on a young harelip patient. Dr. Richardson died later that week.

After graduating from Pennsylvania Women's Medical College, Katharine got on a train west in 1887, buying a ticket for as far as her money would go. She got off in Wisconsin, practiced medicine, married, and moved to Kansas City. Her sister, Alice Berry Graham, recently widowed, soon joined the Richardsons here. The two women officed and the three of them lived together in the Ridge building downtown until construction of their stone house at 121 Clinton Place in the Northeast district was completed. There Mr. Richardson died in 1908, and the two sisters continued in their comfortable home, "filled with simple but beautiful things, and furniture of Katharine's own design." The house is still there.

Dr. Richardson had three loves: she was a "first class furniture designer." In both her home and the basement of Mercy there were fully-equipped carpentry shops. There she and her carpenter made, among other items, all the furniture for Nurse's Hall; she was also a nature-lover, and avid horticulturalist—her funeral was conducted beneath her favorite maple tree on the hospital lawn at Independence avenue and Woodland; but her greatest devotion was medicine and what it could do for children.

Through the years she strove to keep the hospital "human", frequently voicing her concern that "after I am gone, I fear Mercy will become only another institution." During her reign she rode herd on it like a mother tiger, never accepting a penny of salary although she spent four-fifths of her time there.

Dr. Katharine Berry Richardson died June 3, 1933 and was buried in Mt. Washington Cemetery beside Alice, her beloved sister.

129

# Dr. Isaac Ridge

*1825-1907*

## Early Doctor

Dr. Isaac M. Ridge came to Kansas City in June 1848, just shy of 23 years of age, when our town's population stood at 400. He was born July 9, 1825 in Adair County, Kentucky, and graduated from Transylvania University in Lexington. Ridge came here, one of the first graduate physicians to settle in Kansas City specifically to practice medicine.

A year later, the good doctor himself contracted cholera in the 1849 epidemic. But for the timely ministrations of Dr. Charles Robinson of Lawrence, Ridge would have been lost. He survived, and in time repaid his debt in kind when in 1861 Dr. Robinson's life was in peril. It was during a border incident in which Dr. Ridge intervened on Robinson's behalf and saved his life. Dr. Charles Robinson lived to become the first Governor of the state of Kansas.

Perhaps the greatest service Dr. Ridge rendered as a medical doctor in Kansas City, however, was in founding a "pest hospital" on an island in the middle of the Missouri River. There at his own expense, he provided the only means of isolating highly contagious disease victims from the populace and vice versa. His facility served primitively but well into the 1880s, until the entire island was washed away by a changing current in the river.

Dr. Ridge married Eliza Smart, daughter of James Smart, one of the Kansas Town Company's original shareholders, and became an early and sagacious investor in downtown real estate. The first Ridge cottage was built on property between Walnut and Main, 9th to 10th streets, and was torn down to make way for two subsequent multi-storied Ridge buildings.

After serving long and faithfully as City Physician, Dr. Ridge retired from active practice in 1875, devoting himself to his real estate investments, and becoming a millionaire property-owner in the doing.

In 1882, Dr. Ridge began building "Castle Ridge", his commodious home at 2101 Woodland avenue. Constructed in the form of a cross, it stood on 36 hilly acres. Following his death, the site housed the Gilliss Orphans' Home and Armour Home, and later, Western Seminary for Negroes.

Hardy old Dr. Ridge died May 7, 1907, but not before he had diagnosed his own malady and prescribed surgery. At almost 82, he succumbed of "complications and heart failure."

131

# Rev. Nathan Scarritt

*1821-1890*

## Teacher-Preacher

The Rev. Nathan Scarritt was a college-educated teacher-preacher who traveled extensively through Indian country planting seeds of wisdom and faith. In the doing, he became a millionaire real estate investor.

Scarritt arrived in 1848 at 27, armed with a college degree, and ordained as a Methodist minister. He became a canny investor, buying farmland out Northeast in 1862 which left him two million dollars richer when he died 28 years later.

Nathan Scarritt was born in Edwardsville, Illinois on April 14, 1821. He came here "to teach the classics" in this barren outpost at the behest of Thomas Johnson at the Shawnee Methodist Indian Manual Labor School. The Rev. Scarritt spent a lifetime pounding book-learning into young heads at all levels: at early grammar schools in Westport; at a seminary for young women; and at a Bible training school for missionaries.

For all that, the memorable thing about Scarritt is merely his presence here. Half the credit goes to his helpmate, Martha Matilda Chick, who produced their nine children. Originally they lived in Westport, in a tidy two-story frame farmhouse at 4038 Central street (now much-altered as Byers 3 Interiors.) In pre-Civil War years the minister was both anti-slavery and sympathetic with the southerners' dilemma. When in 1862 border incidents and his neutrality made Westport

an unhealthy place to live, the Scarritts moved to their farm.

Their 260 acres lay just above the east junction of today's Cliff Drive and Gladstone boulevard, and in time, the Scarritt name became synonymous with that area. Paths the Scarritt boys used for driving their cows to drink at Scarritt Spring became part of the curvy roadway to Kessler Park and Cliff Drive, and Kessler Park itself is on Scarritt farmland.

In the 1880s Scarritt platted the Melrose Addition from his Northeast acreage, where within ten years palatial mansions sprouted. There he gave each of his children a parcel to build on. At one time 11 Scarritt houses polka-dotted the neighborhood. Most notable, still standing and family-owned is his eldest son's 1898 stone and shingle manse at 3500 Gladstone boulevard, the Scarritt-Royster home.

Nathan Scarritt died at age 69 on May 22, 1890. He had come early, done his job well, raised a large family, prospered, and helped make a silk purse out of this sow's ear we call Kansas City.

# Ruth Seufert

*1897-1975*

Celebrity Series

Ruth Seufert was born an almost-firecracker on July 5, 1897, into a musical family and was trained as a pianist. Interestingly, she parlayed her background and talent not into performing, but into presenting. Is there a gray head in Kansas City for whom "Ruth Seufert Celebrity Series" doesn't ring a bell? And stir memories of the big-name concert talent she brought here?

Ruth Nordberg of Bonner Springs, Kansas, daughter of Swedish violinist Olaf G. Nordberg, became Ruth Seufert when she married the Philharmonic Orchestra's Swedish cellist, Arno Seufert. All her life was inundated with music. Her two brothers played with the old Nighthawks radio orchestra on WDAF, and from the Philharmonic's beginning in the early 1930s, Ruth Seufert was there in the thick of things.

In 1941 when the perennially impecunious orchestra was as usual strapped for funds, she was made business manager. At the end of five years, there was a surplus of $8,000 in their coffers. She appeared to be on the right track until she asked for a one-year contract, and her "resignation" was accepted. That was the spring of 1946.

Ruth Seufert just marched forth and established her own concert management agency. Taking along a portion of the staff from the Philharmonic office, she began booking artists for the fall 1946 season. Among guests appearing in the Music Hall that first precarious year were some really big guns: Metropolitan lyric soprano Eleanor Steber, Puerto Rican pianist Jesus Maria Sanroma, and a violin-piano recital duo of Adolf Busch and Rudolf Serkin. There was Metropolitan Opera mezzo Rose Bampton, French pianist Robert Casadesus, duo-pianists Wittemore and Lowe, and the entire Indianapolis Symphony under Fabien Sevitzky's direction.

From that time for 30 years, Ruth Seufert presented the lion's share of imported "culture" to this town, from Burl Ives to Marcel Marceau. And for most of that time, she attentively fed and watered her artists at the superlative downtown eatery of her friend Max Bretton. (He even named a salad after one of her young artists, Van Cliburn.)

Ruth Seufert died at age 77 on January 25, 1975. Without her dynamism, the celebrity series ground to a halt with a Mark Twain lecture, a ballet, the Vienna Choir Boys, and a ragtime recital of Scott Joplin's music.

135

# Samuel Sosland

*1889-1983*
Publisher

Samuel Sosland's long life began August 4, 1889 near Vilna, Russia, where he was born the second of nine children. From that far-away beginning, Sosland climbed so high on the American ladder of success that it must have amazed even him—as financial journalist, cultural philanthropist, patriarch of an influential family, respected member of both Jewish and Gentile communities and of his business whirl as well.

When father, Henry Sosland, brought his wife and three small sons to Kansas City, they settled in the West Bottoms in a modest home with a dirt floor. There was nowhere to go but up, so that's the route the Soslands took. Sam Sosland's working career began at the nearby stockyards as errand boy for the DAILY DROVERS TELEGRAM, a respected trade publication for stockmen. It was a first glimpse of what was to be his life's work— writing, publishing and making money.

Sam Sosland graduated from old Central High downtown, became a financial reporter, and in 1922 at age 33, he and his brothers David and Sanders began publishing their own trade paper. Theirs, pitched to the grain and milling trade (in which David alone had had experience), was called THE SOUTHWESTERN MILLER.

Now known as MILLING AND BAKING NEWS, this little-known (to the outside world) weekly with a circulation of 6,000 is the Bible of the grain business. For 44 years Sam Sosland was at the heart of it, writing and directing its news coverage with an iron hand. He ruled imperiously, demanding accuracy and fairness, if not outright perfection from everyone including himself. Until his death he was managing editor, serving also as chairman of Sosland Companies Inc., the family-owned holding company.

As patriarch of the Soslands hereabouts, bachelor Sam Sosland was a staunch family man in the old-world sense—and no-nonsense. Since most Sosland philanthropy funnels through a family foundation, which Sam Sosland served as Chairman, he was also an art benefactor of enormous proportions; their gifts to the Nelson-Atkins Museum of Art are legendary. But Sam Sosland's personal high-water mark came in April 1983 when he endowed the post of curator of American Art there with a million dollar gift. When he died, he left the bulk of his multi-million dollar estate to the family foundation for the benefit of mostly local charities. Thus Sam Sosland's climb up the ladder of success proved to be our success too.

Ninety-four year old Sam Sosland was a colorful character who reported for work daily until six weeks before his death on November 6, 1983.

# Helen and Kenneth Spencer

*1902-1982*        *1902-1960*

## Benefactors

Kenneth Spencer began his working life as an already well-to-do third generation coal-mine owner and operator in the mineral-rich Pittsburg, Kansas area. Helen Elizabeth Foresman, his pretty high school sweetheart, entered the scene January 6, 1927 when they married. For 33 years the former KU athlete and his vivacious wife made beautiful music together. It is not facetious to say that he made the money, and she spent it, with impeccable taste and good guidance.

In southeast Kansas the Spencer family coal mines, already big business, metamorphosed into a chemical kingdom. Kenneth Spencer's engineering savvy, his inventions, World War II explosives production, manufacture of chemicals for fertilizer and industry—all teamed-up to make Spencer Chemical Company blanket the midwest. Gulf Oil bought him out in the early 1950s, and made Kenneth A. Spencer rich as Croesus.

It was soon after the Spencers moved to Kansas City that they began leaving their trail of benefactions. In 1949 they created a multi-million dollar charitable foundation. Then they made their alma mater a gift of their English Tudor home in Mission Hills, as the residence for the director of the KU Medical Center here.

When Kenneth Spencer died in 1960, he left an estate in excess of $15 million plus the Charitable Trust, to which Helen Spencer relinquished her interest five years later. That move freed those funds for her giving also, and from then on, giving was her *raison de être*.

Limiting her gifts to Kansas and Missouri, and putting her money where "it would move institutions toward long-range goals", she sallied forth, leaving her tasteful mark on things educational and cultural from here to Lawrence. Locally her generosity ranks with William Rockhill Nelson and William Volker of an earlier era.

With majestic understatement following her eleventh hour gift of $2 million for theatre construction in the Performing Arts Center at UMKC, Mrs. Spencer said, "My late husband and I were very proud to live in the Middle West and hoped to do all we possibly could to enrich this area by the development of its cultural, educational and scientific institutions. Since Kenneth's death, I have tried to carry on and accomplish some of these goals . . . "

Eighty year old Helen Spencer died the day after Valentine's Day 1982, as beautifully as she lived, without illness and without warning, in her own bed in her gracious apartment at The Walnuts.

# Arthur E. Stilwell

*1859-1928*

## Railroad Builder

Arthur Stilwell had railroads in his blood. His grandfather, Hamblin Stilwell, one of the builders of the Erie Canal, had helped build the New York Central. Young Arthur, a mystic who believed in visions, voices, spirits and omens, followed his grandfather's lead.

Stilwell was born October 21, 1859, the sickly son of a well-to-do Rochester, New York family (where grandfather Stilwell was also mayor.) At age 14 Arthur Stilwell apprenticed in printing, and at age 20 came to Kansas City where he worked in a print shop in the West Bottoms which, fittingly, specialized in printing railroad timetables.

In 1888, not yet 30, Arthur Stilwell founded Guardian Trust Company here, a vehicle for financing low-cost housing on an insurance plan. It paid off handsomely, and Stilwell's next stop was railroad-building.

His first, Kansas City Suburban Belt Railway, became the forerunner of Kansas City Terminal Railway. Next came his Kansas City-Independence Air-Line, an interurban to Independence via Fairmount Park, which he built to support the line. Then came the Kansas City, Pittsburg & Gulf, connecting Kansas City to Shreveport and on to Port Arthur, Texas, which was named for him. Stilwell, the youngest railroad president in the country, unfortunately lost control of this winner to his nemesis "the Wall Street interests." After-wards the line went on to become today's big money-making Kansas City Southern.

Arthur Stilwell bounced back in 1900 with his dream road, the Kansas City, Mexico & Orient—his "short route" from Kansas City to the west coast of Mexico. It was 1630 miles as the crow flies, but sadly, trains don't fly. And the craggy mountains and rugged terrain across Mexico together with Pancho Villa and the Mexican Revolution spelled Stilwell's defeat. His investors lost $20 million and Stilwell was forced out. The line went into receivership then, with Kansas City banker William T. Kemper, Sr. named receiver. Years later when oil was discovered along the line's right-of-way, it was Kemper, who held more than 50% of the stock in Stilwell's "old, decrepit and disconnected Orient", who sold out to the Santa Fe for $14 million.

Arthur Stilwell, the visionary who won big on his early schemes, had lost big on his last. Moving to New York, he indulged himself in writing—Christian Science hymns, plays, fiction, political speeches attacking Wall Street financiers, anti-war books, and reputedly some of the worst poetry to flow from a pen. He died September 27, 1928 at age 68 leaving an estate of $1,000. His remains were cremated and according to his wishes, his ashes scattered to the four winds, with a few even wafting back here perhaps.

141

*...ng the tracks of the Kansas City Southern.*

# Clara and Russell **Stover**

*1882-1975*    *1888-1954*

## Eskimo Pie & Stovers Candy

In 1921 the Stovers crashed American big business with an edible brainstorm called the Eskimo Pie—a chocolate-covered ice cream square in a little bag. Fifteen months later they escaped the frenzy it had created with just enough money to buy a bungalow in Denver and go into the candy-making business. From a cottage-industry called "Mrs. Stover's Bungalow Candies" to today's world-recognized Russell Stover Candies is their story.

Russell Stover was born in 1888 in a sod house in northwest Kansas. Clara Lewis was a farm girl too, born six years earlier, and bred in Iowa. They met at the University of Iowa, renewed their acquaintance several years later when he was selling candy (what else?) to the store where she worked. They courted by correspondence, married, moved to Canada (he, still selling candy), returned to the U. S. (she, now making candy), and ultimately to Omaha.

It was there a chap approached Stover with the chocolate-covered ice cream bar idea. Stover parlayed it into the Eskimo Pie sensation so quickly it was rags to riches to almost rags again in little more than one year. After the first mad surge for the novelty, sales settled to a mundane level, and the Stovers bailed out. Reynolds Aluminum ended up with Eskimo Pie, and the Stovers got out with $25,000.

Next came Denver and the infancy of "Mrs. Stover's Bungalow Candies" there. By 1931 the Stovers moved themselves and their now-thriving business to Kansas City. Here they weathered the Depression and the sugar-short World War II years to emerge a multi-million dollar a year enterprise with world-wide sales.

The company's memorable headquarters were downtown at 1206 Main street, and who could forget their sweet-smelling factory with its pastel "garden" office on the fourth floor. Stepping off the elevator, an ersatz bungalow in pink and blue met the eye. A white picket fence surrounded the front yard where the switchboard girl held sway. In a lawn-like area surrounding, the office girls sat at desks on a pink-carpeted expanse. It was all band-box neat and tidy. It was corny too, but so were Clara and Russell Stover, and they never pretended otherwise.

Sixty-six year old Russell Stover died May 11, 1954. Clara Stover survived him by 20 years, carrying on the candy business they nurtured from nothing, until selling out in 1960. She remained to the end in their sprawling Mission Hills mansion, a 26-room showplace at 5805 Mission Drive. There 93 year old Mrs. Russell Stover, known for her business savvy, fluffy hats and early morning swims (until age 88 she swam 30 times daily across her pool) died on January 9, 1975. She's gone, but the candy lives on under the same familiar name.

143

# Robert R. Sutherland, Jr.

*1884-1941*

## Lumber Yards

Robert Robinson Sutherland had four lucrative cash-and-carry lumberyards when he died suddenly just before World War II. Now a garland of 80-plus Sutherland yards reaches across the upper midwest from Omaha to Cincinnati, and the breadth of the Sun Belt from Atlanta to California. As pater familias of three generations now in the empire, he spawned it all in the depths of the Depression with one yard and a lot of gumption.

A nearly-Kansas City native, Robert R. Sutherland was born March 17, 1884, in Garnett, Kansas. From the time he began working for the Belt Line Lumber Company in his late teens, lumber and Sutherland have been one. When he went with Dierks Lumber & Coal Company, that was a double-edged stroke of good luck. He became general manager of that company here, and married Herman Dierks' daughter, Mae, as well.

In 1918 at age 34 Sutherland went out on his own. In Hugo, Oklahoma he opened one garden-variety "house pattern yard", and in the next four years opened four more. He was catering to builders and contractors, when he realized it was oil exploration and *not* home building that was booming in Oklahoma. The real money was in wooden derricks and huge amounts of heavy timber, giant planks and cement. So Sutherland's general lumber yards quickly metamorphosed into "oil field yards", opening and closing as oil came in and petered out.

For seven years these movable yards made it big. Then came the Great Depression. The general economy was going to hell in a handbasket, and on top of all else, oil derricks began converting from wood to steel. As he saw lumber's role phasing out, Robert Sutherland did likewise. With a new concept, "cash-and-carry" in an industry built on credit and delivery, he opened his first new lumberyard in Des Moines in 1932.

There he offered lumber at vastly lower prices while plastering the surrounding area with hand-addressed price lists and circulars. As the lean days of the Depression continued, Sutherland was opening yards in Omaha, Oklahoma City, and, in 1936, here at the stockyards.

Robert R. Sutherland was Kansas City's cut-rate lumber czar. He is remembered as a big, able, energetic outdoorsman. But for those driving south from the Plaza on Ward Parkway in pre-war years, Sutherland is remembered as that sensitive soul whose sprawling yard at the corner of 55th street was ablaze each spring with thousands of red tulips.

At age 57 Robert Sutherland died on November 22, 1941. His widow remained in their Art Deco Louis Curtiss-designed showplace until her death in 1982 at age 94.

145

# Col. Thomas H. Swope

*1827-1909*

## Swope Park

In 1896 seventy year old Col. Thomas Hunton Swope, an early opponent of "all this park foolishness", gave Kansas City one of the largest municipal parks in America. Swope Park, 1350 rolling wooded acres lying four miles southeast of town, made his name famous. But for a time after his death, Swope's name was more famous for the mysterious circumstances surrounding his sudden illness and demise than for his incredible gift.

A Kentuckian born October 21, 1827, Swope was a Yale graduate with money to invest who came west in 1855 as the Kansas Territory opened. At 28 he was one of our decision-makers. At 30, Colonel Swope was a wealthy man, due largely to his early downtown real estate investments.

Exceptionally mild-mannered and self-conscious, Swope was a lifelong bachelor. He lived alone until late in life when he moved into the grand turreted red brick castle of his late brother in Independence. From his sister-in-law's household (redolent of seven nieces and nephews), the frugal millionaire commuted daily by streetcar to his downtown Kansas City office in the New England building until the month before his death.

Swope's last days were preoccupied with how best to bestow his wealth. His real estate alone was worth three and a half million dollars. A sickly solitary soul given to self-doctoring, Swope fell under the spell of a middle-aged doctor who had married one of his young nieces, a suspected "gold-digger" named B. Clark Hyde.

On October 3, 1909, just 18 days short of his 82nd birthday, Col. Swope died suddenly in his sister-in-law's home with Dr. Hyde in attendance, the aftermath of a perplexing, brief and violent illness. The great philanthropist's body lay in state at the Public Library where thousands of mourners paid their respects. Until a tomb could be prepared in Swope Park where he had requested burial, he lay in a holding vault.

Three months after his death, Swope's doctor/nephew-in-law, B. Clark Hyde, came under suspicion, and was charged with murder by strychnine poisoning in "a plot for money." Swope's body was exhumed and an autopsy performed. Three trials, seven years and a quarter of a million dollars later, Hyde went scot-free, his suspected guilt never proven.

Eight and a half years after his death, Col. Thomas B. Swope was at last laid to rest in Swope Park. On April 8, 1918 he was buried high on a hill amid a forest of trees, overlooking his gift to Kansas City. There he lies beneath a Greek temple of white granite, guarded by a pair of stone lions, solitary in death as in life.

147

# Sallie Casey and William B. Thayer

*1856-1925* *1852-1907*

## Merchant & Art Patron

The Thayers were Kentuckians born mid-nineteenth century, an educated, cultivated, monied couple. William Thayer's name lives today, the "last name" in Kansas City's late-lamented department store, Emery, Bird, Thayer & Company. Sallie Casey Thayer is known to art lovers for her collection, now the nucleus of KU's Spencer Museum of Art in Lawrence.

Thayer came to Kansas City in 1871 at age 19, joining Bullene, Moore, Emery Company as bookkeeper. Thirteen years later he was made a partner, and their head financial man. In 1885, the store's name was changed to include his.

In 1906 the socially prominent, well-traveled, art-conscious Thayers built "Sevenoaks", a 15-room mansion at 4570 Warwick boulevard, present site of Oak Hall apartments. Their impressive cut stone manse exuded all the amenities of a wealthy and influential couple of educated tastes. Just a year after it was built, William Thayer died at age 54.

Sallie Casey Thayer, born on Valentine's Day 1856, was 51 when her husband died. She was a human dynamo, energetic, tireless, and bright. Art and history were her consuming interests, so small wonder that in widowhood she became a serious art student, world traveler, and discerning collector.

She studied at the Chicago Art Institute and traveled the world; amassed a 600-volume personal library, a prodigious collection of Coptic textiles, Japanese prints and Indian baskets, American quilts, European glass and exemplary contemporary paintings, and whatever else caught her educated eye.

Mrs. Thayer was opinionated and outspoken, and openly disdainful of the backward condition of the arts here. "Now the pioneer city has made its money, it ought to cultivate its mind", she vowed. And that was her mission.

As early as 1912 she began ragging the City Fathers to build an art museum to which she would donate her collection. Their response was vague disinterest. She approached the University of Missouri, whose indecisiveness infuriated her. Finally she made overtures to the University of Kansas, where she hit pay dirt. On June 2, 1917, after long and delicate negotiations, Sallie Casey Thayer presented her collection to KU—5,000 objects filling two freight cars found a make-shift home on The Hill.

Another nine years were to pass before her life's work would find a permanent resting place. Sallie Casey Thayer died at age 69 on September 10, 1925. Nine months later, on June 8, 1926 the red sandstone Spooner Library opened as the Spooner Thayer Museum, displaying her incredible collection, a star in KU's firmament. In 1977 the new Helen F. Spencer Museum of Art opened and Mrs. Thayer's collection became its heart.

149

# Dr. Benoist Troost

*1786-1859*

## Town Father

Most visitors to the Nelson-Atkins Museum of Art have seen the 1859 George Caleb Bingham portraits there of Dr. and Mrs. Troost. Regarded as pure vintage Bingham, they portray Dr. Troost as a cheerful, florid, robust Dutchman in his early seventies. Mary Troost is softly round, rosy-cheeked, a sweet-faced matron, ten years the doctor's junior. Thus the Troosts appeared the year of the doctor's death, and 13 years before his widow's. Both were early and important shapers of our town.

Dr. Troost, born November 17, 1786 in Bois Le Duc, Holland, was a graduate physician who served as hospital steward in the Army of Napoleon. Arriving here in the early 1840s, Dr. Troost soon suffered the death of his first wife. Five years later in 1846 Troost married "the sprightly young widow, Mrs. Mary Kennerly", favorite niece of the wealthy and prominent bachelor William Gilliss.

Dr. Troost was physician, city father, and early entrepreneur. At the sale of lots of the Town Company of Kansas in 1846, he bought five! In 1849 as the California gold rush peaked, Troost and his wife's uncle built the town's first brick hotel. Called the Gilliss House, it boasted "46 apartments roomy and modern" at the corner of Delaware and Wyandotte. Later called the Free State hotel, the escape of Kansas Governor Reeder from it, disguised as a laborer, is one of the celebrated local incidents of the Civil War.

From 1850 Dr. Troost served as a trustee of the Town; was defeated in the first mayoral election of 1853 but elected to the city council; was a major backer of the first newspaper; and an incorporator of the Chamber of Commerce. On February 8, 1859, the wise and good doctor died at age 72. He was buried in the old Catholic Cemetery beside his first wife. Later, both were moved to Mt. St. Mary's Cemetery where Mary Troost erected a monument inscribed to *Benoit* L. G. Troost, M.D., and Rachel Tage Troost.

Mary Ann Gilliss Troost lived another 13 years, and spent much of that time establishing and perpetuating a memorial to her late uncle. William Gilliss had left his considerable fortune to Mrs. Troost, and she, in turn, devoted most of it to creating the Gilliss Orphans' Home at 11th and Charlotte in his memory.

Mary Troost was visiting a friend near Philadelphia when she contracted smallpox, and died on December 27, 1872. Fear of the disease and its contamination lead to her swift burial at St. Martin's cemetery in nearby Marcus Hook, Pennsylvania. Thus the gentle second Mrs. Troost lies east, while the good doctor and his first wife lie here, in the town they all helped shape.

151

# Col. Robert T. Van Horn

*1824-1916*

Editor

Col. Robert Thompson Van Horn came to Kansas City early and stayed late. Past 91 when he died, Van Horn's able finger was in almost every pie from his arrival here at age 31 until his death almost 61 years later. Kansas City's first lawyer by profession, a journeyman printer by trade, Van Horn came here not successful at much of anything.

Of Pennsylvania-Dutch ancestry, Robert Van Horn was born July 14, 1824 in Indiana County, Pennsylvania to the blue-blood of patriotism, with Revolutionary War ancestors on both sides. He arrived here July 31, 1855 and by October of that year became the city's first crusading editor of our only newspaper (buying the ENTERPRISE and renaming it WESTERN JOURNAL OF COMMERCE). In 1860 he served as postmaster, in 1861 as the town's sixth mayor; in 1864 he was elected to Congress and became the leading spokesman/strategist during Kansas City's railroad-luring period. He was our supreme civic booster and dedicated wound-healer. The worst possible crime, he vowed, was to "injure the city's prospects." Philosophically he was pro-Union; politically he was a Whig cum Democrat on his way toward Radical Republicanism in his last years.

But editor Van Horn was first and foremost a "builder": a charter member of the Chamber of Commerce, an incorporator of the Frisco Railroad, and an outstanding combat officer bearing Kansas City's destiny uppermost in his mind. Although he was never one of the land-owning gentry of this town, he was a charter member of its decision-making circle. Editorially he put the brightest face possible on events bearing on Kansas City's destiny. He was adroit in handling the touchy issues raised by the border troubles; the essence of decisive ability and political adaptability. And it helped that he was a warm personal friend of Presidents Lincoln and Grant, and an acquaintance of every president from the Civil War on until his death.

In 1896 he built what he called his country seat in Independence, "Honeywood", a spacious comfortable rock house at Winner road and 15th street (site of today's Van Horn High School). It was there that wise old Robert Van Horn died at age 91 on January 3, 1916. The itinerent editor had seen Kansas City from its infancy endure growing pains, survive bitter War years, burgeon in the land booming 1880s, retrench at the turn of the century, and burst into bloom before World War I. Throughout, his faith in the future of this place never dimmed. He was a truly good man who helped make us what we are today.

153

# William Volker

*1859-1947*

## Philanthropist

William Volker alias "Mr. Anonymous of Bell Street" alias "First Citizen" of Kansas City was an extremely modest, enormously wealthy home furnishings tycoon. He became patron saint of the University of Kansas City, father of the Board of Pardons and Paroles, the Helping Hand's guardian angel, the Board of Education's loyal longstanding member and anonymous source of funds, Research Hospital's major benefactor, and unrecognized donor of thousands of smaller gifts as well.

On April 1, 1859 William Volker was born into a prosperous household in Hanover, Germany. At age 12, German-speaking William together with his family arrived in Chicago where he attended school, learned English and helped his family do likewise. At 17 he went to work for a picture-frame manufacturer-jobber, and Volker's die was cast.

When the company's owner died, 20 year old William Volker was made manager, and almost immediately the enterprising young man began casting about for a new business location. One with less competition, an ample supply of walnut lumber, and good rail connections. In 1882 he found it all in Kansas City. Here was a busy rail center blossoming with industries and at the peak of a building boom.

Volker bought out the Chicago picture frame business, relocated it here, and expanded its line to include roller shades and linoleum. The newly enlarged William Volker Company located at 6 West 3rd street, and from there his "little window shade business" grew into a national giant.

Once established here the bachelor-businessman sent to Chicago for his family—parents, sisters and brother. To house them all he first built a substantial farmhouse at 29th and Jefferson streets in Penn Valley. Then in 1890 Volker purchased "Roselawn", a comfortable three-story, 12-room brick and shingle house at 3717 Bell street on a woodsy two acres. Here, his old-world mother raised a vegetable garden, kept a cow and chickens, and his father planted roses.

In 1911, 52 year old William Volker married. Returning from his honeymoon, Volker announced he had put one million dollars in his wife's name "so she could take care of him when he grew old . . . he intended to give the rest away." And he did just that, spending ten million dollars on philanthropy here in the next 36 years. Yet this slight, self-effacing man could walk down the streets of Kansas City and rarely be recognized—which suited him just fine.

When William Volker died at age 88 on November 4, 1947, Kansas City lost a man of grace, warmth and concern. He had the money and the wisdom to help in big ways and small.

155

# Seth Ward

*1820-1903*

## Frontier Trader

Mention Seth Ward's name and Ward Parkway comes to mind. That, or his handsome antebellum Ward house on 55th street. But history buffs know Ward as Indian trader, frontiersman, Westport banker, fur trapper, contemporary and friend of William Bent, as well as prosperous sutler of Fort Laramie.

Seth Edmund Ward was born of English ancestry March 4, 1820 in Camden County, Virginia. In 1834 at age 14 when apprenticed as a laborer to a family in Indiana, he ran away and headed west. In Independence he joined a trading outfit that traveled as far as the Green River in Colorado. And there for seven years, from 1838 until 1845, he "lived with the Indians", taking an Indian wife and siring four children.

In 1845 Ward returned to Westport purchasing wagons and supplies, and continued trading with the Indians until the mid-1850s when he was appointed sutler (government supply officer) at booming Fort Laramie on the Oregon-California Trail in Wyoming. There at the busiest post on the frontier he made a fortune, buying travel-worn oxen and excess supplies from gold-seekers headed west with their over-loaded wagons, and reselling them to new arrivals in short supply.

In 1860 Ward married the divorced daughter of Colonel John Harris of Westport, Mary Frances McCarty, returning to Kansas City in 1871 to

settle. Here Ward acquired the farm from the estate of his friend and fellow trader William Bent. Ultimately reaching from State Line to Wornall road, 51st to 55th street, it contained Bent's two-story farmhouse which was incorporated into the present Ward-Bent house at 1032 West 55th street—a rosy red brick mansion, designed by early Kansas City architect Asa Beebe Cross. Its 14 rooms with eight fireplaces and nine porches stand not far from the site of the final day's fighting of the Battle of Westport.

In 1897 Ward's east pasture became the Kansas City Country Club's first golf course, and in 1926 the southeast 80 of his original farm became today's lovely Loose Park.

Seth Ward spent the last 32 years of his life in Kansas City, farming and banking—a tame finale for a restless westering man. A southern sympathizer and unswerving Democrat, Ward vowed not to shave "until the Confederacy won its freedom." When he died December 9, 1903, he was a wealthy, distinguished 83, wearing a full white beard he'd been nuturing for 41 years.

# Charles E. Whittaker

*1901-1973*

## Supreme Court Justice

Charles Evans Whittaker, Kansas City's only claim-to-fame on the Supreme Court of the United States was appointed by President Eisenhower and sworn in March 25, 1957.

Whittaker, who rose from boy fur trapper to a seat on the highest court in the land, was born on a farm south of Troy, Kansas on Washington's birthday, 1901. Appropriately his parents gave him the same Christian names as Charles Evans Hughes, that (other) great American statesman and jurist who was appointed to the Supreme Court in 1910.

While attending rural high school, Whittaker, who "started working hard as a child and never stopped", earned $800 fur trapping. Although he had not yet graduated from high school, that lordly sum covered his tuition to the Kansas City School of Law in 1920. Attending law school three days a week and Manual High two, Whittaker also began working as a clerk in the law firm of Watson, Gage & Ess. And that was the beginning of the law career of Charles Whittaker, highly respected lawyer of the old school. "Success depends on honesty, and work backed up by high ideals and morals."

From 1954 until his appointment to the Supreme Court, Whittaker sat on all three tiers of the Federal bench, serving with a thoroughness that seems almost corny today. A lifelong Republican, strict constructionist, and strong defender of judicial restraint, he vigorously attacked the concept of "peaceful civil disobedience." Warning against a populace obeying only "good laws" but not "bad ones", he cautioned, "Who will umpire?"

Judge Whittaker was simplistic, if not downright square, in the eyes of his detractors. A lawyer's lawyer, Charles Whittaker was never really happy on the Supreme Court, nor with life in Washington, D. C. Pressure of the work and contentious infighting of the court weighed heavily on him. He valued friendships on the court with Justice Felix Frankfurter and Chief Justice Earl Warren (with whom he seldom agreed), but retired after five brief years a weary and disillusioned man.

Returning to Kansas City in 1962, Whittaker spoke publicly of his concern that law and order had become an option, and enforcement of it passé. His disenchantment showed until finally he ceased taking a public stand when no one seemed to be listening.

In a summing-up shortly before his death at age 72 on November 26, 1973, Justice Whittaker said, "You cannot enforce criminal laws against determined criminal people with a feather duster." He was a rare jurist who dared say the unpopular.

159

# Wight & Wight

*1874-1949*      *1882-1947*

## Architects

Brothers Thomas and William D. Wight were partners in one of Kansas City's most prestigious architectural firms of the early to mid-1900s. Most of our institutions of stature from that period bear their stamp: the Nelson-Atkins Museum of Art, Kansas City Life Insurance building, Jackson County Courthouse, City Hall, old Children's Mercy Hospital, Federal Courts building, downtown Post Office, Municipal Courts building and Police Headquarters, Southeast High School, Pickwick hotel and the Pickwick building, and even Col. Thomas Swope's Memorial in Swope Park. Wight & Wight's neo-classic designs permeated Kansas City's architecture into the 1940s.

The brothers Wight of Scottish descent were born in Halifax, Nova Scotia, and came to Kansas City after working in the highly-regarded firm of McKim, Mead & White in New York and Boston. Thomas Wight, elder of the two, was born September 17, 1874. At 17 he answered an advertisement in the Boston newspaper for a "boy" at McKim, Mead & White, who at the time were designing the Boston Public Library.

When the firm closed its Boston office upon completing that project, Thomas Wight went along to their New York office. Ten years there, and one year off for travel and study abroad followed.

In 1904 Thomas Wight came to Kansas City to become a partner here with his friend Edward

T. Wilder. Wilder & Wight's design for the First National Bank building at 10th street and Baltimore avenue in 1906 was a high-water mark. In 1911, younger brother William D. Wight joined their practice, and five years later when Wilder retired, the firm name became Wight & Wight.

William D. Wight, eight years his brother's junior, was born January 22, 1882. His architectural background largely duplicated his brother's— ten years with McKim, Mead and White in New York, and one year of European travel and study, then Kansas City.

Wight & Wight's building designs were never frivolous but "remained imbued with classical spirit long after others flirted with experimentation." Their hallmark was propriety and permanence. Even the few houses they reluctantly designed reflect that same solid classicism like the residence at 1028 West 58th street.

For 45 years the brothers Wight made their architectural statement in Kansas City. William D., the younger brother, died October 29, 1947 at age 65; Thomas died October 6, 1949 at age 75. Their impact on Kansas City's facade is rich, significant and lasting.

161

# Willard Winner

*1849-1929*

## North Kansas City

Forty-two year old Willard E. Winner was one of the big losers in our real estate bust of 1890. Alternately known as "The Jay Gould of the West" and simply "crazy as a loon", Winner was a visionary-developer hopelessly ahead of his time.

Willard Winner was born in Fairfield, Iowa May 4, 1849, and came here with his family about 1860. Twenty years later as real estate began booming, he began buying, and in 1883 organized Winner Investment Company.

Certain that Kansas City's growth was towards Independence, in 1886 he bought 2400 acres out east, building Washington Amusement Park (today's Mt. Washington Cemetery) and the steam-powered railway which served it and the area. Intercity—Blue Valley, Centropolis, Sheffield—all were largely Winner's creations, as was broad, winding Winner road which bears his name.

In 1887 Winner began looking north for development possibilities. Forming North Kansas City Improvement Company (predecessor of today's NKC Development Company), he bought almost 20,000 acres north of the river and began building a bridge (to replace the ferry) to get there. In North Kansas City he envisioned plant sites and low-cost worker housing, and in two years' time, high-flying Willard Winner sank more than $4 million dollars there.

Alas, the Oklahoma Territory opened with great fanfare about the same time. Venture money and footloose folks chased rainbows there rather than to North Kansas City. By 1890 Kansas City's real estate bubble burst, and although Winner held on longer than most, even *his* credit eventually dried up. When it did, Winner's dreamed-of Missouri River bridge (he'd already sunk the substructure and nine cut stone piers!) and train station project halted. Years later his river crossing came into being when the Armour, Swift and Burlington railroad picked up Winner's land, finished his bridge (albeit slightly to the west), and opened it as the ASB. In 1911, the old ferry boat to Clay County was finally retired.

Meanwhile on April 18, 1891 Willard Winner's assets had been assigned to bankruptcy. The man who was Kansas City's Postmaster at 17, built its first electric trolley line at 26 (on 5th street between Main and Locust), and developed vast areas both east and north of the city before he was 40, was a king-sized loser at 42.

But expansive Willard Winner regrouped, reorganized, and became respectable once more. After 1920 he was referred to as a "solid citizen with leaping imagination and glittering dreams." On the eve of the Great Depression, September 2, 1929, 80-year old Willard Winner died, bowed but still brimming with plans for Kansas Ciy.

# Kathryn Winstead

*1893-1967*

Winstead's

Winstead's is a hamburger joint you either love or loathe, or else you've never been there and have no opinion. Food-funnyman Calvin Trillin regards Winstead's hamburgers as the best in the world. A lot of other hamburger-commentators not nearly so funny think it's pretty ordinary. Whatever your ground, Winstead's is a Kansas City institution. Its hamburgers *are* legendary; its streamlined cream-colored terra cotta building, a landmark; and its founders—two sisters named Winstead (plus one brother-in-law/husband)—almost obscure.

Kathryn Winstead was born in Jacksonville, Illinois in 1893. Thirty-four years later with the help of her sister Nellie, and Nellie's husband Gordon, Kathryn Winstead founded the first Winstead's drive-in in nearby Springfield, Illinois. In bleak old 1932 a "drive-in" meant just that: driving your car into a restaurant parking lot, giving your order to a car-hop, being served on a little tray hooked over your partially rolled-up car window, flashing your headlights for tray pick-up afterwards, tipping the cutie who responded, and driving off in a blaze of youthful exuberance.

After that trial balloon in Springfield, Miss Winstead opened a drive-in in her hometown of Jacksonville, Illinois, and then one in far distant Sedalia, Missouri. Finally in 1940 it was Kansas City's turn. At 101 Brush Creek Boulevard, just east of the Plaza and the old Country Club streetcar tracks, she opened in a slick, boxy, Moderne little building, with service both inside and out.

Winstead's unchanging kid-simple menu featured steakburgers, spoon-thick chocolate malts lovingly called "Frosties", and superb limeades sporting a healthy scoop of lime sherbet cocked rakishly on one edge of the glass. With that fare Winstead's tantalized the teen-agers of the Fabulous Forties. For a dozen years until Kathryn Winstead's retirement in 1952 her inimitable drive-in was THE place to go after a date, on a date, or for a date in the south part of town.

Kathryn Winstead died at age 74 on June 21, 1967, reportedly leaving an estate of $340,000, which is a lot of fries and Frosties. Two years later Winstead's on Brush Creek was sold, expanded, remodeled, and "branched" (North Kansas City and Overland Park.) Through it all the status has remained mostly quo. The menu's the same, the expansion tolerable, the remodeling sensitive. All in all, the spirit of its founder remains intact, and except for the demise of its "curb service", Winstead's is pretty much now as then—for better or for worse.

# Fred Wolferman

*1870-1955*

Wolferman's

For almost 85 years Wolferman's was without peer. From 1888 when Fred Wolferman's father mortgaged the family home at 1521 Charlotte for $750 to buy a bankrupt grocery at 317 East 9th street, their name has meant "Good Things To Eat."

Father Wolferman emigrated from Germany, settled in Milwaukee and there son Fred was born September 13, 1870. Early in the 1880s he gathered up his family and moved here, opening a vinegar plant in the West Bottoms which was only mildly successful. Then came the 1888 grocery store purchase, and the family's course was set.

With a delivery horse named Fanny and a new-fangled telephone (number 638) for taking orders, young Fred, who had had visions of becoming a doctor, became instead our premier grocer. Gross receipts the first day were only $5.65, but Wolferman's prospered, and in 1895 moved uptown to 1108 Walnut street. There they opened a meat market; a restaurant soon followed; and in 1904, a bake shop. In 1909 a fire and subsequent rebuilding resulted in the revered seven-story structure which became their downtown base—store, restaurants, plant and office.

As the city expanded southward, Wolferman opened his first suburban store in 1912 at 59th street and Brookside boulevard amid truck gardens and cornfields. There in a structure housing a saddle repair shop, livery and movie house, Wolferman's opened. In 1950 a stunning new windowless Spanish-style store complete with clock tower replaced all that.

Seven years later in 1919, Wolferman's opened at 40th and Main streets, to be replaced in 1937 by a smart new store adjacent to the southwest corner of Armour boulevard and Main street. Built of reinforced concrete to a modified Maltese cross floor plan, it was a gem of Streamline styling. Both new stores reflected the daring of art-loving Fred Wolferman and of architect Edward Tanner.

Wolferman's on the Country Club Plaza opened in 1923 on the northeast corner of Wyandotte and 47th streets. Locally there were five suburban Wolferman's, one in Tulsa, and 60 associate stores in four states. Their incomparable bakeries turned-out feather-light classics; Twin Sycamore Farms produced fresh breakfast-makings; their private labels ranged from tinned foods to liquor and spelled quality. From salads to sausage, from dressings to dairy products, Fred Wolferman said, "We only buy what we cannot make better." And his "better" was always the best.

Fred Wolferman died at age 85 on October 2, 1955, and by 1972 Kansas City was out of "Good Things to Eat." Now an abbreviated version operated by a grandson is in Fairway.

# Herbert Woolf

*1880-1964*

## Woolf Brothers

Herb Woolf's name means many things—all of them top-drawer. It means Woolf Brothers fine clothing stores. And race horses, especially his Derby-winning Lawrin. And the Loews Midland Theater downtown. It means the herd of Herefords he sold to William Randolph Hearst for his San Simeon ranch. And the 200-acre Woolford farm at 82nd street and Mission road where the Barn Players originally performed in its horse barn. But most of all, Herb Woolf's name means style. Verve. Panache.

Herbert M. Woolf was born October 11, 1880 at his family's home at 913 Locust street. The Woolf brothers, his father and uncle, had moved down river from Leavenworth the year before to open a men's furnishings store here. In Leavenworth since 1868, they had specialized in tailor-made shirts for Army officers at the Fort, and double-breasted red flannel underwear which tied at the ankles. Here in a narrow three-story building at 557 Main street they opened a men's store, with laundry and shirt factory upstairs.

In 1909 they opened at their present location on the corner of 11th and Walnut streets. In 1912 young Herb Woolf became manager; and three years later, president. With unerring good taste he undertook stylish re-do's and expansions downtown; opened five out-of-town branches; and in 1958, a store on the Country Club Plaza.

While Herb Woolf's real business was retailing, horses were his love from childhood.

And in 1933 he went from saddle horses to race horses in a happy fluke. On a rainy day with Herb Woolf the only bidder, he bought one of the great sires in American racing history. For $500 he bought Insco, the sire out of whom came fabled Lawrin—born, bred and buried on Woolf's farm.

Lawrin was Herb Woolf's and Kansas City's winner in 1938 when that big beautiful copper-brown three-year old colt (ridden by 23 year old Eddie Arcaro) won the 64th running of the Kentucky Derby in 2 minutes 4⅘ seconds. Lawrin lived to be 20, siring Historian. Now Lawrin, his sire Insco, and his son Historian all lie beneath the monument at Woolford Farm.

Herb Woolf took lots of flyers that made him and Kansas City look great. He was an investor with Barney Allis in the venerable Muehlebach hotel. Through his friendship with Marcus Loew, the palatial Midland theater was built in downtown Kansas City, and the Uptown and Plaza theaters too. (Woolf subsequently became a partner in a 57-house movie chain.) With his love of Herefords and horses, he served the American Royal loyally and long. He loved everything he got into, and he got into everything that fascinated him. When he died September 22, 1964 at age 83, Kansas City lost one of its "greats."

# John B. Wornall

*1822-1892*

## Gentleman Farmer

On October 1, 1972, just 11 days short of the 150th anniversary of John Wornall's birth, his restored southern farm mansion opened as a house-museum. It had then stood vigil for 114 years on the northeast corner of Wornall road and 61st terrace. History had marched past its front door since 1858—the year the gracious red brick two-story Greek Revival house was first occupied by John Wornall and his bride of four years, Eliza.

John Bristow Wornall, a Kentucky-born Scotsman first saw the light of day October 12, 1822. He came here with his family 21 years later from Shelbyville, all settling in a small four-room house on a farm 2½ miles southeast of Westport. His father paid John Calvin McCoy $2500 for the 500-acres which, in the progression of things, soon became young John Wornall's.

In 1850 at age 28, he married Kentucky-born Matilda A. Polk who died one brief year later. In 1854 he took a second wife, 18 year old Eliza Johnson, daughter of the Rev. Thomas Johnson of the nearby Shawnee Methodist Indian Manual Labor School. And it was for her that he built the stately white-pillared Wornall house. Passing in front was the main county road leading south from Westport to New Santa Fe, some ten miles distant, and to the vast frontier beyond. The Oregon Trail. The Santa Fe Trail.

Here gentleman John Wornall became a serious and successful farmer. On this farm which stretched from State Line to Main street, from 59th to 67th streets, he cropped wheat, corn, oats, hay and 100 acres of Kentucky bluegrass. And he did very well.

Wornall, a slave-owning southern sympathizer, and his young Eliza lived there even as the Civil War heated up. On occasion the house was ransacked; Jayhawkers occupied it for one eight-day period; and during the bloody Battle of Westport it served as hospital to troops of both sides. But when Eliza's father, the Rev. Johnson was murdered in January 1865, the Wornalls moved from their remote farm into the city. Six months later, Eliza died bearing her second surviving child.

The following year, 44 year old John Wornall, father of two young children, married a third time, to 20 year old Roma Johnson, Eliza's cousin. Although their wedding ceremony was performed in the parlour of the Wornall farmhouse, it was not until eight years later that they returned there to live.

On November 24, 1892 John Wornall died at age 70. Roma lived another 41 years, all but one in the family-owned home. In 1964 the Jackson County Historical Society purchased and restored it as a house-museum reflecting the lives of prosperous farm families in western Missouri in the 1850s and 1860s. Truly, "old John Wornall builded us a fine house."

171

# Thank You

From the outset the Missouri Valley Room staff at the Kansas City Public Library bore up under my presence for weeks on end, amid voracious requests for "more!" Marj Kinney, Peg Smith and Virginia Wright, thank you, thank you, thank you.

My gratitude also to Kathy Sherman who tends the UMKC Library's Snyder Collection. And my sincerest appreciation goes to the willing folks at all the cemeteries we stalked; they have been tolerant, helpful and so interested.

Special thanks also to David Chow of Reversal Systems for his consultation and advice on film selection and processing of the photographs in this book. Thanks, indeed, to Jerry Bledsoe and Mike O'Neill, our patient and excellent typographers of Uppercase and Typographics. But most of all, to Jane and Bob Flynn, our cemetery cohorts of thirty years standing, bless you!

*Wilda Sandy*
*June 1984*

# References

Spaulding, Charles C. *Annals of the City of Kansas.* Kansas City: Van Horn & Abeel, 1858. Reprinted by Frank Glenn Publishing Co., 1950.

Haskell, Henry C., Jr. and Fowler, Richard B. *City of the Future, A Narrative History of Kansas City, 1850-1950.* Kansas City: Frank Glenn Publishing Co., Inc., 1950.

Garwood, Darrell *Crossroads of America, The Story of Kansas City.* New York: W. W. Norton & Co., Inc., 1948.

Brown, A. Theodore *Frontier Community, Kansas City to 1870.* Columbia: University of Missouri Press, 1963.

Brown, A. Theodore and Dorsett, Lyle W. *K.C., A History of Kansas City, Missouri.* Boulder: Pruett Publishing Co., 1978.

*Kansas City, A Place in Time.* Kansas City: Landmarks Commission, 1977.

Ehrlich, George *Kansas City, Missouri, An Architectural History, 1826-1976.* Kansas City: Historic Kansas City Foundation, 1979.

Whitney, Carrie Westlake *Kansas City, Missouri, Its History and Its People.* 3 vols. Chicago: S.J. Clarke Publishing Co., 1908.

Fowler, Dick *Leaders of Our Town.* Kansas City: Burd & Fletcher Co., 1952.

Ray, Mrs. Sam *Postcards From Old Kansas City.* Kansas City: Historic Kansas City Foundation, 1980.

Rhodes, Richard *The Inland Ground, An Evocation of the American Middle West.* New York: Atheneum, 1970.

*Where These Rocky Bluffs Meet.* Kansas City: The Chamber of Commerce, 1938.

Native Sons Archives scrapbooks, Missouri Valley Room, Kansas City Public Library.

Clipping files of the Missouri Valley Room, Kansas City Public Library and of the Snyder Collection, UMKC Library.

# Cemeteries

Boone-Hays Cemetery, northwest of 63rd street and Brooklyn avenue
Calvary Cemetery, 6901 Troost avenue, 523-2114
Elmwood Cemetery, 4900 Truman road, 231-0373
Forest Hill Cemetery, 6901 Troost avenue, 523-2114
Lincoln Cemetery, 8604 East Truman road, Independence, 252-8175
Mt. Carmel Cemetery, 9331 East 55th street, Raytown, 353-4196
Mt. Moriah Cemetery, 10507 Holmes road, 942-2004
Mt. St. Mary's Cemetery, 2201 Cleveland avenue, 241-7663
Mt. Washington Cemetery, 614 Brookside drive, Independence, 252-4141
Rose Hill Cemetery, 712 East 69th street, 363-1050
Shawnee Indian Cemetery, 59th terrace east of Nieman road, Shawnee
Shawnee Methodist Mission Cemetery, Johnson drive, Fairway, 262-0867
Sheffield Cemetery, 6200 Wilson road, 231-6191
Swope Memorial Cemetery, Swope Park, end of Swope Memorial drive
Union Cemetery, 227 East 28th terrace, 471-0883

## St. Louis

Bellefontaine Cemetery, 4947 West Florissant avenue, 314-381-0750
Calvary Cemetery, 5239 West Florissant avenue, 314-381-1313